HILLBILLY COOKBOOK

© David Richards

BY David Richards

Yo' Favorite Hillbilly Recipes & Fixins

HILLBILLY COOKBOOK

BY David Richards

Yo' Favorite Hillbilly Recipes & Fixins

Whosoever Press books may be ordered through booksellers or by contacting:

Whosoever Press

P.O. Box 1513

Boaz, AL 35957

www.whosoeverpress.com

1-256-706-3315

Because of the dynamic nature of the Internet, any web addresses or links contained in this book may have changed since publication and may no longer be valid. The views expressed in this work are solely those of the author and do not necessarily reflect the views of the publisher, and the publisher hereby disclaims any responsibility for them.

Front cover imagery created and provided by Emily Richards.

Front Cover Image © David Richards

Printed in the United States of America

Whosoever Press date: 10/15/2016

I WANT TO SAY A SPECIAL THANK YOU TO MY NIECE EMILY RICHARDS FOR CREATING THE FRONT COVER CHARACTER FOR MY BOOK!

Hillbilly Cookbook

Hello Fellow Hillbillies, Country Folk, and City Slickers,

I am David Richards, and I grew up in the Appalachian Mountains of West Virginia, where the love of God, Family, Friends, and Good Eatin' is the way of life...I have heard all of the hillbilly jokes and name calling that comes from being a true hillbilly from the mountains. I don't care what you call me as long as you call me when it's time to eat. That's why I am putting this cookbook together. If you're going to call me over for supper I want the best grub and fixins that a hillbilly can eat. I hope you enjoy these recipes for many years to come.

Be Blessed,

Hillbilly Dave

Hillbilly Grace

Before we hillbillies put grub on our plate and stuff our face...we take time to say Grace. So take the time to say your Grace, and here's a little prayer for you to say...

God is Good, God is Great, thank ya for the grub that's on my plate. Help this Hillbilly to be content...Whether it be a coon, possum, or rattlesnake, Lord let taste like a big juicy steak..........Amen!

Let's Eat!

Hillbilly Dave

I would like to dedicate this book to the coal miner's and their families. I want to thank each and every miner for their hard work and dedication. These people are the heart of the Appalachian Mountains that makes this nation strong with the energy of coal. I want to say R.I.P to the miners that gave their lives in the coal mines and that God will bless their families with a coal miner's grace.

Hillbilly Dave

Yo' Favorite Hillbilly Recipes & Fixins
Hillbilly Guide

Turn to your favorite recipe or fixin' and enjoy a taste of hillbilly heaven....

Hillbilly Dave

Hillbilly Humor

Growin' up a poor hillbilly in the Appalachian Mountains, my baloney didn't have a first name...So I called it Hillbilly Round Steak.

Hillbilly Dave

Hillbilly Temps

Maw sure was glad when she got electricity in the old log cabin...she went out and bought her a new stove to cook them hillbilly vitals, but she needed help in knowin' how to set the temperatures on that new oven, so paw had it all figured out and wants to pass it on to you.

Oven Temperatures

Temperature (Degrees)	Term (Heat temp)
250-300 degrees	Slow cookin'
325 degrees	Moderately Slow
350 degrees	Moderate
375 degrees	Moderately quick
400 degrees	Moderately Hot
425-450 degrees	Very Hot
475- 500 degrees	A Hillbilly Scorcher

Like Maw tells Paw... If you can't handle the heat, stay out of the kitchen!

HILLBILLY MEASURING GUIDE

NOW YOU DON'T HAVE TO USE YOUR FINGERS AND TOES TO FIGURE OUT HOW TO MEASURE UP TO GREAT COOKING.

A few grains = Less than an 1/8 tsp
Pinch = as much as can be pinched between tip of finger and thumb
Speck = Less than 1/8 tsp.

3 tsp. = 1 TB

2 TBS = 1/8 cup

4 TBS = 1/4 cup

5 TBS + 1 tsp = 1/3 cup

8 TBS = 1/2 cup

10 TBS + 2 tsp + 2/3 cup

12 TBS = 3/4 cup

16 TBS = 1 cup

2 cups = 1 pint

4 cups = 1 quart

2 pints = 1 quart

2 cups or 4 sticks of butter = 1 lb.

1/2 cup + 2 TBS = 5/8 cup

3/4 cup + 2TBS =7/8 cup

1 oz. = 2TBS fat or liquid

4 oz. = 1/2 cup

8 oz. = 1 cup

16 oz. = 1 pound

2 cups of fat or lard = 1 pound

2 cups of granulated sugar = 1 lb.

2 2/3 cup of powder sugar = 1 lb.

2 2/3 cup of brown sugar = 1 lb.

4 cups of sifted flour = 1 lb.

Hillbilly Dry Meat Rub

It's not rocket science, just Hillbilly know-how

1 cup of Paprika

3 ½ Tbs. of sugar

½ tsp. Onion Powder

½ tsp. Black Pepper

Mix it all together for a great rub!

Hillbilly Marinade

2 Cups of ketchup

6 Tbs. Brown Sugar

5 Tbs. White Sugar

1 ½ tsp. Paprika

1 ½ tsp. Ground Mustard

1 ½ tsp. Black Pepper

1 ½ tsp. Onion Powder

1 cup of water

½ cup of Apple Cider Vinegar

Mix all the ingredients together bring to a boil...Reduce heat and simmer for 1 hour...while simmering, add half of a lemon's juice.

HILLBILLY CAKE BAKING TIP

Do you want to make your cake taste like it came fresh from a hillbilly bakery? Well, just follow these simple steps…

1. Read the direction on the cake mix box
2. Add one cackler (EGG) or Two for even richer cake
3. Replace the oil or lard with melted butter and double the amount
4. Replace water with an equal amount of milk
5. Mix and bake like your cake mix box tells you

   Now ya know how to bake like a Hillbilly Pro…

Billy Bob's Brunswick Stew

1 lb. hamburger meat

½ lb. pork sausage

1/3 cookin' oil

1 can mater paste

2 medium taters-diced

1 Tbs. salt

2 Tbs. sugar

2 quarts of water

1 can of butter beans

1 can of cream-style corn

___Don't have to be from Brunswick to stew things up_____
Brown hamburger meat and sausage in oil; add mater
paste, taters, salt, sugar, water and butter beans; cook
until taters and beans are tender. Add corn and cook for
10 minutes longer. Add water a desired. Corn bread can
be invited to this show.

Count to three meatloaf

2 lbs. Hamburger Meat

1 ½ cups of evaporated milk

2 envelopes of dry onion soup mix

_____No fuzzy math here, just count to three_____

Preheat oven to 350 degrees. Mix all ingredients well in a 2 ½ quart bowl. Place mixture in an ungreased shallow baking pan; shape into a loaf. Bake for 1 hour at 350 degrees: Yields 8 big slabs of meatloaf.

Put some good old mashed taters with it and some corn on the cob and you will make some happy hillbillies...

AUNT UNICE'S APPLE-TATER MEAT LOAF

1 lb ground beef

1 medium tater- grated

1 medium apple- grated

$\frac{1}{2}$ cup of fine bread crumbs

$\frac{1}{4}$ cup of onion- chopped

$\frac{1}{4}$ cup of bell pepper - chopped

$\frac{1}{2}$ tsp salt

$\frac{1}{2}$ tsp black pepper

1 egg

_____Gather them apples & Taters_____

Mix all ingredients. Form into a loaf-Put into a foil lined loaf pan. Bake at 350 degrees for 1 hour.

A great hillbilly tip when cooking any kind of meatloaf....line loaf pan with sliced bread, put meatloaf on the bed of bread, and cook as normal...the bread keeps the bottom from burning, and it acts as a sponge and absorbs all the grease...cut the meatloaf and serve and discard the bread...Now, aren't ya glad you bought this cookbook?

BACON CHEESEBURGER MEATLOAF

1 Lb. of ground chuck

10 slices of bacon, cooked & crumbled

1 (8oz.) package of sharp cheddar cheese, grated

2 large eggs lightly beaten

¼ cup bread crumbs, toasted

¼ cup of mayonnaise

1 Tbs Worcestershire Sauce

¼ tsp salt

¼ tsp of black pepper

1/3 cup of ketchup

2 Tbs of prepared mustard

1 (3oz.) can of French Fried onions

_____LET'S LOAF FOR AWHILE_____

Preheat oven to 350 degrees

In a large bowl, combine the ground chuck and next 8 ingredients- mixing it well.

In a small bowl, combine ketchup and mustard. Stir ¼ cup ketchup mixture into meat mixture. Reserve remaining ketchup mixture

Press meat mixture into a 9x5x3 inch loaf pan, or shape into a loaf and place on the middle rack. Spread remaining ketchup mixture over loaf and Bake for 40 minutes. Top with French Fried Onions: bake another 10-15 minutes or until meat is no longer pink.

Hillbilly helpful hint: line your loaf pan with slices of bread and lay the loaf on top of the bread. This will keep the bottom from burning and will absorb the grease. Discard the bread after cooking.

Hillbilly Shrimpalaya

1 cup of cooked shrimp

2 cups of cooked elbow macaroni

1 ¼ cup o cooked ham or canned luncheon meat (cubed)

1 large can of tomatoes

½ bread crumbs

2 strips of bacon (diced)

½ cup of minced onion

1 tsp. mince garlic

½ cup of green bell pepper (diced)

1 tsp salt

2 Tbsp grated Parmesan cheese

2 Tbsp of butter

_____This hillbilly ain't a lyin' about this Shrimpalaya_____

Sauté bacon till crisp; add onions, bell pepper and garlic until tender; add tomatoes and salt then add macaroni, ham and shrimp; pour into a baking dish or pan. Combine crumbs, cheese and butter and sprinkle it on top. Bake at 350 degrees for about 30 minutes. Makes enough for four Hillbillayasa

COAL MINER'S SKILLET DELIGHT

1 lb. hamburger meat

4 Tbs. canola or veggie oil

1 onion- chopped

2 Tbs. chili powder

1 Tbs. black pepper

1 cup rice, uncooked

1 can of kidney or pinto beans

1 can of maters

$\frac{1}{4}$ tsp garlic salt

2 tsp salt

_____Grab a Skillet!_____

Brown hamburger meat and onions in oil and cook at medium heat- add in the rest of the ingredients and cook on high until boiling hot, reduce heat to low and cook for 25-30 minutes longer. Time to dig in...

Great with cat head biscuits or fried cornbread

Hillbilly Beef & Rice Dinner

1 lb. Ground Beef

1 cup of Minute rice

1/3 onion- diced

1 Tbs. chili powder

1 (10oz) bag of frozen corn

1 green bell pepper- cut up

1 can of tomato sauce

½ cup of water

1 cup of shredded cheddar cheese

_____Beef up your hillbilly and fill him full of rice_____
Brown hamburger meat and onion together in a large skillet. Add chili powder, corn, bell pepper, tomato sauce and water. Cover and bring to a boil. Stir occasionally; reduce heat and add rice and cover again for 5 minutes or until rice is done. Sprinkle cheese and let melt. Time to serve.

15

Hillbilly BBQ Weenies

8-10 of your favorite weenies

½ cup of BBQ sauce

2 Tbs. brown sugar

2 Tbs. of prepared mustard

2 Tbs. of diced onions

2 Tbs. water

_____It's Weenie Q time_____

Place weenies in a casserole dish. Mix remaining
ingredients together; pour over weenies and bake at 375
degrees for 15-20 minutes. Feeds 4 Hillbillies

The weenies are the star of the show

HILLBILLY HASH

1 Lb of ground beef, possum, or coon

2. Tbs. butter

$\frac{1}{4}$ cup onions- finely chopped

$\frac{1}{4}$ cup of bell peppers -finely chopped

1 tsp salt

1 tsp chili powder

$\frac{1}{4}$ cup of molasses

$\frac{1}{4}$ cup of prepared mustard

2 Tbs. Worcestershire sauce

1 large can of maters

1 cup of raw rice (white or wild brown)

_____Hash it out_____

Melt butter-sauté onion and bell pepper and cook until tender but not brown- add hamburger meat and brown. Put in all the other ingredients to the meat. Cover- reduce the heat and simmer until rice is fully cooked. Feeds 8-10 starvin' hillbillies.

HILLBILLY HAMBURGER STEW

1 ½ lb of hamburger meat

½ cup onion chopped

2 Tbs. of canola or veggie oil

1 cup of ketchup

1 cup of water

2 cups of celery- cut in 1" strips

4 medium carrots – cut in 1" pieces

4 medium taters- quartered up

2 tsp salt

1/8 tsp of pepper

_____I say, Stew this!_____

Brown hamburger meat and onions in oil/ add remaining ingredients, simmer covered, for 1 hour or until veggies are tender. / add, more water if stew becomes too thick.

6-8 servings

GOES GREAT WITH SOME CORNBREAD

Hen House Chickin-n- Dumplins

2 lbs Chickin (chicken)

2 cups of chicken broth (water from cooked chicken)

1 cup of milk

$\frac{1}{2}$ cup of flour

2 Tbs. melted butter

1 can of cream of chicken soup

$\frac{1}{4}$ tsp salt

$\frac{1}{2}$ tsp of black pepper

_____Hey little chickin the dumplins are fallin'_____

Place chicken in a large pot and cover with water; Cover and cook over medium heat for 1 hour. Remove chicken from pot and save the water for chicken broth. Shred chicken in small pieces and place in a casserole dish; Mix Flour, milk and butter and pour over chicken. In another bowl mix broth, soup, salt and pepper and pour it over the other stuff in the casserole dish...DO NOT STIR! Bake at 350 degrees for 1 hour. Let it sit for a few minutes before serving.

Don't let that rooster in the hen house...the dumplins will be jealous...

Granny's Green Rice

3 cups of rice- cooked

½ cup of butter- melted

1 small onion- finely chopped

1 (4oz) can of green chilies- chopped

1 cup of ground parsley

2 eggs

1 cup of milk

2 cups of cheddar cheese- grated

_____Turnin' green with Granny's rice_____

Mix all the ingredients; put into a casserole dish. Bake at 350 degrees for 40-45 minutes. Feeds 10 hungry hillbillies.

Make your hillbilly friends green with envy for some of this wild rice

Aunt Millie's Baked Mac-n-Cheese

2 cups of elbow macaroni - cooked

8 oz. of Velveeta cheese- cut into ½ cubes

1 cup of milk

¼ cup of butter- divided

¼ cup of flour

½ cup of shredded cheddar cheese

6 round crackers- crumbled as crumbs

_____Aunt Millie is Mac-n-the cheese_____

Preheat oven to 350 degrees. Melt 3 Tbs. of butter in a sauce pan over medium heat. Whisk in flour; cook for 2 minutes, stirring constantly. Gradually stir in the milk. Bring to a boil; cook and stir for 5 minutes or until thick. Add Velveeta cheese; cook for 3 minutes, stir constantly. Stir in cooked macaroni. Place in a greased casserole dish, sprinkle cheddar cheese on mixture. Melt the remaining butter; toss with crumbs. Sprinkle on top of casserole. Bake for 20 minutes or until it is heated all the way through

Good enuff to Mac your Granny!

Aunt Wilma's Weenie Pie

8-10 jumbo weenies –sliced ½ inch thick chunks

½ cup of chopped onions

¼ cup of chopped green bell peppers

½ cup of chopped celery

2 ½ Tbs. of flour

3 Tbs. canola oil or olive oil

1 ¼ cup of milk

1 Tbs. Worcestershire sauce

1 tsp salt

1/8 tsp black pepper

1 ½ cup of mashed taters

_____Weenie Up!_____

Sauté weenies, onions, green pepper, and celery in oil; blend in flour. Slowly stir in milk; bring to boil. Cook until thickened, stirring constantly. Add Worcestershire sauce and seasonings; blend well. Pour into greased casserole dish. Top with mashed taters. Bake at 350 degrees for 30 minutes.

Aunt Bertha's Black Bean Dip

1 package of chorizo sausage-castings removed

1 can of black beans-rinsed and drained

1 jar of chunky salsa -medium or hot

1 tsp lime juice

1 tsp cumin

3 Tbs. fresh cilantro-chopped

1 bag Shredded Cheddar Cheese

1 bag of tortilla chips...scoop size

Beans, Beans good for the heart...the more you eat them the more you....Well, you know!

Brown chorizo sausage in a large skillet over medium-high heat-stirring until sausage is well broken up into small pieces and done. Drain well. Stir in salsa, black beans, cumin and lime juice, cook until it's thoroughly cooked. Sprinkle with cilantro and cheddar cheese. Serve warm with tortilla chips.

Hillbilly Weenie-Q

1 pack of 8 count jumbo weenies

½ cup of chopped onion

1 Tbs. of cooking oil

1 ½ cups of ketchup or your favorite B-B-Q sauce

2 Tbs. of pickle relish

1 Tbs. sugar

Dash of salt & pepper to taste

Hot cooked rice

_____Best Weenie B-B-Q in the hollow_____

Cook onions in oil until tender. Stir in ketchup, ½ cup of water, relish, sugar, salt & pepper. Cut weenies in small size chunks. Add to sauce; simmer, covered, until weenies are heated through, about 10-12 minutes. Serve over the cooked hot rice and enjoy! You can put this in a jar and can it for later use…Yum.

Po' Boy's Pork-n-Bean Surprise

1lb. hamburger meat

1 large can of Pork-n-Beans

2 cups of medium noodles (cooked)

1 large can of tomatoes (drained)

Apple wood smoked bacon (strips)

Salt & Pepper

Brown sugar

1 small onion (diced)

$\frac{1}{2}$ tsp. dry mustard

_____Let's surprise them Pork-n-Beans_____

Brown hamburger meat with onions, salt, pepper, dry mustard. Alternate layers of beans, meat and noodles twice. Sprinkle a little brown sugar between layers. Spread the drain tomatoes over the top and sprinkle with salt and pepper. Cover with strips of uncooked. Sprinkle some more brown sugar on top of bacon. Bake at 350 degrees uncovered for 45 minutes or until bacon is crisp and cooked. Dat'll make a Po' Boy happy!

Mex-a-Billy Fiesta Fling

1 lb. of hamburger meat

½ tsp. pepper

1 tsp. chili powder

¼ cup of chopped onions

1 large jalapeno pepper-seeded and chopped

1 tsp. salt

½ cup of water

1 cup of Mexican cornbread mix

2 cups of cooked rice or Spanish rice

1 can of tomatoes w/ green chilies (Do not drain)

_____Have a hillbilly wild fling with this thing_____

Brown hamburger meat in a large skillet add cooked rice, tomatoes, salt, pepper, onions, jalapeno pepper, water and chili powder; Cook until liquid is absorbed. Top with corn bread batter made with 1 cup of mix. Bake at 425 degrees for 25 minutes.

COUSIN ERNIE'S -ENCHILADA PIE

1 lb hamburger meat

1 chopped yellow onion

1 can of cream of mushroom soup

2 cans of diced green chilies

1 can of crushed maters

1 can of mater sauce

Veggie or canola oil

1 pack of corn tortillas

1 pack (2 cups) shredded Colby Jack Cheese

_____Preheat Your Oven 350 degrees_____

Brown the beef and onions together & drain. In a sauce pan cook the soup, chilies, crushed maters and the mater sauce-Add the browned hamburger meat and simmer on low heat. In a frying skillet heat a little cooking oil (Veggie or Canola) and cook the tortillas until they are warm and soft. Put 4 of the warm tortillas in the bottom of a casserole dish and top with $\frac{1}{2}$ meat mixture. Sprinkle with $\frac{1}{2}$ of the cheese- Repeat layers with the remaining tortillas, meat mixture and cheese. Bake for 30-35 minutes.

Country Time Crockpot Lasagna

1 lb. hamburger meat

1 box of lasagna noodles

1 jar pf spaghetti sauce

1 ½ cup ricotta cheese

1 ½ cup of shredded mozzarella cheese

2 Tbs. parmesan cheese

_____Git out yo' crock pot, Maw_____

Brown hamburger meat and drain. Place 1 cup of spaghetti sauce in the bottom of a crock pot. Spread 1/3 cup of meat on top of noodles; Spread ¾ cups of ricotta cheese over meat. Add another layer of uncooked noodles, 1/3 meat mixture, and the remaining ricotta cheese and ½ cup of mozzarella cheese. Place another layer of uncooked noodles, 1/3 meat mixture, and the rest of the mozzarella cheese and sprinkle the Parmesan cheese over top. Cook on low for 4 hours...add some good garlic bread, a salad and enjoy the country crock pot meal...

Country Boy Swiss Steak

1.5 to 2 lbs. of round steak, cut in serving size pieces

1 cup flour (You won't use all of this, but need it to dredge each piece in to cover)

1/2 tsp. seasoned salt

1/2 tsp. garlic salt

1/2 tsp. black pepper

1/4 cup vegetable oil

1 medium size sweet onion, diced

1 green bell pepper, diced

1 32 oz. can of diced stews tomatoes

1-2 cups water

1 Tbs. beef bouillon granules

_____ Head to the Swiss Alps and never leave the farm_____

Dredge each piece of round steak in a the flour. Heat the oil in a heavy deep skillet with a lid or if you have a cast iron Dutch oven, that is perfect for this. Place the round steak in the oil. Sprinkle with the seasoned salt, garlic salt and black pepper. Brown on both sides- Remove to a plate when brown. The steak won't be cooked, just browned. Add the onion and bell pepper to the pan and sauté in the drippings from the meat, loosening any pieces of flour that have stuck to the pan. When they are slightly tender, add the steak back to the pan. Pour the tomatoes, undrained over all. Add 1 cup water and the beef bouillon. Bring up to a bubble and then reduce to simmer. Cover and simmer for at least 1 1/2 hours. About every thirty minutes, stir this from the bottom of the pan, because it does tend to stick....especially if you are cooking it on too high heat. It needs to cook low and slow. Add the other cup of water as needed as it cooks and thickens. The flour from the meat will thicken the tomato gravy that meat cooks in as it simmers.

Country Gal's Carrot Pie

Like we say in the mountains; don't knock it 'til you try it...

2 cups of thinly sliced Carrots
1 cup of water
¼ tsp salt
1 cup of milk
¼ cup of butter or margarine
Pecans to decorate

½ tsp nutmeg
½ tsp of cinnamon
1/8 tsp ginger
½ cup of sugar
2 eggs
9 inch Pie Shell

_____Carrots will make a Blind Hillbilly see_____

Cook carrots till tender and blend until pureed. Beat eggs lightly, and carrots, milk, sugar, butter, spices, and salt; Pour mixture in the pie shell and bake 45 to 50 minutes in a 375 degree oven. Top with pecans to make it look pretty and add to the taste. Enjoy!

HILLBILLY FRIED PICKLES

1 (16 oz.) jar of dill pickle slices
1 cup buttermilk
6-7 drops of hot sauce
1 cup self rising flour
1 cup cornmeal
1 tsp. Cajun seasoning
1/2 tsp. black pepper
1/2 tsp. garlic powder
oil for fryin

_____Pucker Up!_____

Drain the jar of pickles in a colander. Spread the pickle slices out on a double thickness of paper towels to get the liquid off of them as much as possible. When they are fairly dry, mix the buttermilk and hot sauce in a bowl and place the pickle slices in it. If you don't drain them first, the buttermilk won't adhere to the slices. Combine the flour, cornmeal and seasonings in a shallow dish. Remove the pickles and dredge them in the mixture, making sure to cover each slice. Drop a each slice in a deep fryer with oil heated to around 375 degrees. Make sure your oil is hot enough, but not smoking. You can use vegetable oil, canola oil, or peanut oil. If you don't have a deep fryer, you can use a heavy pan with high sides on the stove. The pickles will float to the top if your oil is good and hot. Turn each one over to brown both sides. Use a slotted spoon or tongs to remove them when they are brown to a paper towel lined plate. Serve immediately with ranch dressing!

Hillbilly Fish Sandwich

Fish Sticks -your favorite brand

American Sliced Cheese

Lettuce

Pickles- Dill chips

Onion- slice thinly

Thousand Island dressing

Ketchup

Hamburger Buns- Large ones

_____Gone fishin'_____

Cook fish sticks as directed on package; Place a piece of American cheese on bun, then put 4-5 fish sticks on next, top it with lettuce, pickle, onion, ketchup, and Thousand Island dressing...put the top of bun on and enjoy a great catch!

Hillbilly Faheetas (Fajitas)

Where this Hillbilly is from, we say and spell it Faheetas not Fa-jit-as

1lb. of chicken breast -cut into strips

2 Tbs. cooking oil

2 tsp chili powder

1 ½ tsp of cumin

½ tsp garlic powder

½ tsp of oregano

4 tsp seasoning salt

1 (15oz.) Rotel maters and green chilies

½ red bell pepper-cut into strips

½ green bell pepper-cut into strips

1 medium onion -sliced into strips

_____Hillbilly gonna Faheeta some grub_____

Preheat oven to 400 degrees. Place chicken in greased
13x9 baking dish. In a small bowl combine oil, chili powder,
cumin, garlic powder, oregano and salt mix well and put it
evenly over chicken. Add Rotel, onions and bell peppers on
top. Bake uncovered for 20-25 minutes or until chicken is
fully cooked.

Hillbilly Crescent Burgers

1lb. Hamburger Meat

2 cups of Shredded Cheddar Cheese

Couple of drops of Worcestershire Sauce

1 package of Onion Soup Mix

1 Can (Roll) of Crescent Rolls

1 tsp Pepper

_____Paw, is dat the Burger that looks like the moon? _____

Preheat oven to 350 Degrees

Brown and drain hamburger meat

In medium bowl- mix hamburger and rest of the ingredients

(reserve $\frac{1}{4}$ cup of cheese for topping)

Add a heaping spoon full of meat mixture to the large end of

the unrolled crescent roll – roll up and seal edges

Sprinkle with cheese on top

Bake 15 minutes until golden brown.

Hillbilly Caviar

2 cans of black eyed peas

1 can of black beans

1 bell pepper- chopped

2 cans of Rotel Tomaters (Hot or mild)

2 cans of whole kernel corn

Green onions- diced

½ bottle Italian dressing

_____Po' Boy's Caviar_____

Mix beans, black eyed peas and corn together and heat in microwave for 2 minutes or until hot. And in rest of ingredients and stir it up and serve on some crackers. You can also put it over a nice hot baked tater with a dab of sour cream, salsa, or a sprinkle of Parmesan cheese.

Now, don't you feel like a rich Hillbilly?

Hillbilly Cajun Stew

3 packs of Little Smokey Sausages

2 cans of kidney or pinto beans

3 onions- chopped

2 large cans of mater sauce

4 bell peppers-chopped

2 large jalapenos- seeded and chopped

1 tsp Cajun seasoning

Salt & Pepper to your taste

_____Oooh, how 'bout dat Cajun stew_____

Put all the ingredients in a large pot. Simmer for 2 hours. Add water as needed while cookin' Serve over bed of rice or noodles.

Don't have to be from the bayou, but it will taste like you are

Hillbilly Buffalo Wangs

24- Chicken Wangs (wings for you city folks) 12 Drumetts and 12 flats.

1 cup of melted butter

4 Tbs. of your favorite hot sauce

3 Tbs. red wine vinegar

Canola, Veggie or Peanut Oil (for fryin')

_____Flyin' Hillbilly Style with some good wangs_____
Get your table top fryer out and fill it up with your favorite oil at 360 degrees... Deep fry them wangs for about 9 minutes per batch (don't over fill the fry basket so the wangs won't stick together. Drain. Melt butter and stir in hot sauce, and vinegar; mix well. Put wangs in a large bowl and pour butter mixture on wangs and toss around to coat wangs evenly. Serve with your favorite dippin' sauce and celery sticks.

Hillbilly Gumbo

1-3lb chicken-cut in serving pieces

½ onions- finely chopped

4 cups of cooked Okra, sliced

¼ -red bell pepper- finely diced

1 ½ cups of maters (Tomatoes)

1 cup boiled rice (fully cooked)

3 cups of boiling water

1 ½ tsp of salt

1 tsp Cajun seasoning

_____Jumbo your Gumbo_____

Sprinkle the chicken chunks with salt & Pepper; dredge with flour. Fry in veggie or canola oil. Remove chicken from fryin' pan. Sauté onions in the oil left in pan. Add okra, pepper, and Cajun seasoning; cook slowly for 15 minutes-Add chicken, maters, water, and salt Cook slowly until chicken is tender. Add rice the rice. Stir it up and serve it hot!

Uncle Zack's Zucchini Crisp

1 lb of Zucchini or Squash

¼ cup of shredded Parmesan Cheese (Heaping)

¼ cup of breadcrumbs (Heaping)

1 Tablespoon of Olive Oil

¼ Kosher salt

Freshly ground pepper to taste

¼ tsp of crushed red pepper for a hillbilly kick (Optional)*

_____Git Warm & Crispy_____

Preheat oven to 400 degrees- Slice zucchini or squash in ¼ inch rounds and toss with olive oil to coat well

In a wide bowl or plate combine breadcrumbs, parmesan cheese, crushed red pepper*, salt and pepper. Place rounds in mixture and coat both sides-pressing to adhere - Place in single layer on a baking sheet-sprinkling the rest of the mixture over the slices

Bake 25 minutes until golden brown- do not flip over slices, they will brown on both sides.

Uncle Fred's Freezer Pickles

3 ½ cups of thinly sliced cucumbers

2 small onions-sliced into rings

1 Tbs. salt1 cup sugar

½ cup of white vinegar

3 Tbs. water

_____COOL AS A CUCUMBER!_____

Combine first 3 ingredients in a large bowl; set aside.
Cook sugar, vinegar, and water in a saucepan over medium
heat, stirring until sugar dissolves. Pour over cucumber
mixture. Cover and Chill for 48 hours….Spoon evenly into
half-pint jars or freezer containers; seal label and freeze
pickles up to six months Thaw in refrigerator before
serving. Make sure to use thawed pickles within a week.

Hillbilly Ham & Egg Bake

6 hard boiled eggs (chopped)

4 cups of cooked ham (diced in small bite size pieces)

¼ cup of flour

3 Tbsp. butter

2 tsp. curry powder

1 large can of evaporated milk

1 package of herb-seasoned croutons

_____Ham & Eggs getting' a hillbilly tan_____

Preheat oven 325 degrees. Melt butter in medium sauce pan; remove from heat and slowly stir in flour and curry powder; blend in milk and cook over medium heat while stirring often until thickened (sauce). Place 1 cup of ham in bottom of baking dish; add 3 hard boiled eggs and add 1/3 portion of the flour-curry sauce and repeat with ham, eggs, and flour curry sauce in layers. Add the remaining ham, egg and flour-curry sauce. Top with croutons and bake for 25-30 minutes. Feeds up to 8 bakin' hillbillies...

Hillbilly Coating for Chicken

This is the Hillbilly Fried Chicken recipe

1 Whole Chicken- Cut up

3 Beaten Eggs

4 Tbs. Oil

(For Coating)

1 tsp. Thyme	2 cups of flour
1 tsp. Oregano	$\frac{1}{2}$ tsp. garlic
salt	$\frac{1}{2}$ tsp. onion salt
1 tsp. Tarragon	4 tsp. paprika
$\frac{1}{2}$ tsp. celery salt	1 tsp. pepper
2 $\frac{1}{2}$ tsp. salt	1 tsp. poultry seasoning

_____Spice dat yard bird up right_____

Sift all coating ingredients and place in large plastic bag

Coat each piece of chicken (first) in beaten egg- then with

flour mixture in the bag-coating each piece completely.

Heat oil in large skillet-brown chicken in oil slowly-uncovered

Once brown- cover skillet and keep frying on a very gentle

heat (low to medium heat) until fully cooked

Place on paper towels to drain excess oil

Uncle Bud's Porcupine Meat balls

1 lb. of ground beef (No porcupine was harmed)

1 can of mater soup

$\frac{1}{4}$ cup of raw rice

1 cackle berry (Egg) slightly beaten

$\frac{1}{4}$ cup onion minced

2 Tsp parsley dry or minced

1 tsp salt

2 Tsp. of veggie or canola oil

1 small clove of garlic- minced

1 cup of water

_____Put ya a Porcupine on your plate_____

Mix $\frac{1}{4}$ cup of mater soup, meat, rice, egg, onion, parsley, and salt...Shape into 16 meatballs about 1 $\frac{1}{2}$ inches in diameter...Brown in oil with the garlic...blend remaining soup and water- pour over browned meatballs, cover and simmer about 40 minutes or until rice is tender. Serve hot! Or throw them babies on a bed of noodles to get the full hillbilly effect.

Dat will dress up a plate of spaghetti

Countrified Corn Chip Pie

1lb. Hamburger Meat

1 large can of Chili

1 can of kidney beans or chili beans

1 bag of your favorite brand corn chips (King Sized)

1 lb. of Velveeta cheese cubed and melted

1 large jalapeno pepper (seeded and diced)

_____Get all Countrified for some crazy pie_____

Preheat oven to 350 degrees. Brown hamburger meat & drain in large skillet; pour in canned chili (or you can make homemade chili for a much better taste) and beans in with meat and heat thoroughly. Arrange corn chips, chili & bean mixture and cheese in layers in large baking dish. Bake at 350 degrees for about 5 minutes or until cheese is melted and serve immediately...feeds 4 Countrified Folks

We ain't crazy, we just Countrified!

Hillbilly Baked Beans

1 lb. hamburger meat

½ lb. of pork sausage (mild or hot)

1 can of tomatoes

2 cans of pork-n-beans

¼ cup or BBQ sauce (Smokey flavored is great)

2 Tbsp vinegar

½ cup each of onion, celery and green pepper (chopped)

1 garlic clove (chopped)

1 Tbsp mustard

½ cup of brown sugar

_____When it come to beans, hillbillies know best!_____
Sauté onions, pepper, celery and garlic in a large skillet; Add ground beef and sausage; brown and drain; add rest of the ingredients except for the beans and simmer for 10 minutes then add the beans and mix it well, and put in a baking dish and bake for 45 minutes at 350 degrees.

Sugar Hollow Sausage & Bean Supper

1 lb. of your favorite hot or mild sausage

1 can of Pork-n-Beans

$\frac{1}{4}$ cup chopped onions

1 cup of chopped apples

2 tbsp. of plumped raisins

Dash of cinnamon

_____Come and visit Sugar Hollow for supper_____

Fry sausage-drain and remove from skillet. Reserve two tablespoons of the sausage grease. Add onion to reserved grease in skillet and cook onions until soft. Add apples and raisins and continue to cook. Add sausage, beans and a dash of cinnamon when apples are almost done; simmer for 10 minutes.

Feeds up to 6 Sugar Hollow guests…Y'all come on!

Hillbilly Weenie & Noodle Doodle

1 package of your favorite weenies

½ chopped green bell pepper

½ cup of chopped celery

½ cup of chopped onion

2 chopped pimentos

1 package of noodles (cooked)

1 can cream of mushroom soup

Bread crumbs or butter crackers

_____Hillbilly Doodle & Noodle Your Weenies_____

Cut weenies in small chunks and combine with veggies: add cooked noodles and soup. Place in casserole dish. Top with the bread crumbs or crushed butter crackers. Bake at 350 degrees for 45 minutes. It will doodle up six plates worth.

Dat will make your weenie doodle for a noodle...

Back Woods Beef & Cheese Stew

1 large can of beef stew

1 ½ cups of all-purpose flour

¼ cup of butter

2 tsp. baking powder

1 ½ cups of milk

1 cup of grated cheddar cheese

1 tbsp. on onion flakes

1 tbsp. sugar

_____Down in the back woods for some of dat stew_____
Melt butter in a square baking dish in the oven. Combine remaining ingredients except for the beef stew in a large mixing bowl; stir until blended. Pour over melted butter. Pour beef stew over mixture. Do not stir. Bake at 350 degrees for 1 hour. Feeds 6 back woods hillbillies…Hee Haw, Y'all!

The Southern Sloppy Samiches

1lb. hamburger meat

1lb. sausage (mild or hot)

2 cups of ketchup

1 bell pepper (chopped)

1 onion (diced)

2 tsp. minced garlic

1 Tbsp. brown sugar

2 Tbsp. of yellow mustard

$\frac{1}{2}$ tsp. of your favorite hot sauce

$\frac{1}{4}$ tsp. black pepper

1 cup of water

Pack of large hamburger buns

_____Let's get all sloppy the southern way_____

Mix hamburger meat and sausage and brown it in a large skillet. Drain. Add the bell pepper, onions and garlic and cook another 5 minutes, then add in the ketchup, mustard, brown sugar, hot sauce and pepper and stir it all together. Turn the heat down to low and add the cup of water and let it simmer for 20-25 minutes....Put them on a big bun and top it off with pickles or coleslaw. Man, let's get messy.

49

Hillbilly Upside Down Burger Bake

1lb. Hamburger Meat

¼ cup of chopped onion

1 tsp. salt

½ tsp. chili powder

½ cup of ketchup

1 can of whole kernel corn (undrained)

1 package of cornbread mix (prepared but not baked)

_____Flip your burger upside down_____

Combine first 5 ingredients in a large skillet, breaking up the hamburger meat as it browns. Push hamburger meat Around the edge of the skillet and pour the corn in the center: pour corn bread mix over top of the hamburger meat and corn. Bake at 425 degrees for 25 minutes. Let it cool for at least 5 minutes. This will feed 6 upside down hungry hillbillies

Po' Boy Pizza Burgers

2 lb. hamburger meat

1 cup of mozzarella cheese

1 tsp of Oregano

1 jar of pizza sauce

8 hamburger buns

_____It's a Po' Boy's Pizza on a bun_____
Combine hamburger meat, cheese and oregano. Mix well
and shape into 8 patties; about 3" thick. Fry in a large
skillet or put 'em on the grill. Cook 6-8 minutes until
burger are done. Pull out the buns and slap a burger on it
and top it off with pizza sauce...Feeds 8 Hungry Hillbillies

Forget the delivery!

PAW'S WILDER THAN A MOUNTAIN GOAT

RICE & SAUSAGE

1 lb. of good country sausage (Hot or Mild)

2 medium onions - chopped

1 pkg. wild rice, cooked and drained

$\frac{1}{2}$ pt. of whippin' cream

1 can cream of mushroom soup

2 $\frac{1}{2}$ cups chicken broth

$\frac{1}{2}$ tsp. of oregano

1 tsp of salt

1 cup of chopped almonds

_____Take a walk on the wild side of the rice & sausage_____

Sauté sausage and onions; add to cooked wild rice. Add soup, cream, chicken broth, and seasoning...Top with almonds, Bake at 350 degrees for 35-40 minutes:

This will feed a large hillbilly family. Wee Doggie, Dig in Y'all

Uncle Ollie's Okra Fritters

1 cup of thinly sliced okra

1 egg, beaten

½ cup chopped onion

½ cup of chopped maters

¼ cup of all-purpose flour

½ tsp. salt

½ tsp. curry powder

¼ tsp of black pepper

_____Feed your critters some of these fritters!_____
Combine all the ingredients in a large mixing bowl, stirring well. Drop mixture by tablespoon into hot canola or veggie cooking oil, cooking until golden brown, turning once. Place on paper towel to drain. Enjoy with your favorite dippin' sauce.

OLD GRANNY'S GOULASH

2 Lbs of hamburger meat

2 large white onions- chop 'em babies up

3 cloves of garlic- chopped (Hillbilly breath freshener)

3 cups of water

2 (15 oz.) cans of mater sauce

2 (15 oz.) cans of diced maters

2 Tbs. of Italian seasoning

3 Bay leaves

3 Tbs. soy sauce

1 Tbs. seasoning salt

2 cups of macaronis, uncooked

_____Git ya pot ready Maw_____

In a Dutch oven, brown your hamburger meats while breaking the meat up into small pieces, then drain off the grease. Throw in the garlic and onions in the skillet and sauté until them little babies are tender (about 4 min.) Add the 3 cups of water with the mater sauce, diced maters, Italian seasoning, bay leaves, soy sauce, and seasoned salt. Stir dat mixture up well. Put a lid on the pot and cook for 20 minutes. Add the macaronis and stir it all up...put the lid back where it belongs-on the pot and simmer for 25-30 minutes...Take off the stove and remove the bay leaves and allow the pot of goulash to sit about 25 minutes to settle down before serving. Bring out the salad and bread sticks...

MAW'S MAKE-BELIEVE BARBECUE

1 lb. ground beef

½ bell pepper- finely chopped

1 tsp salt

¼ tsp pepper

1 cup of milk

½ cup of bread crumbs

1 egg- slightly beaten

1 can cream of mater soup- undiluted

1 pack of hamburger buns

_____Slap them fixins together and fool the family_____

Do not brown beef. Mix all ingredients: pour into large glass baking dish. Bake 3 hours at 250 degrees/ Stir every 30 minutes. Serve hot on hamburger buns

Maw-Maw Minnie's Salsa Turkey Burger

1 lb of ground Turkey

½ cup of seasoned bread crumbs

1 cup of chunky salsa

Salt & pepper to taste

Canola or Veggie oil

8 count of seeded hamburger buns

_____Gobble This Down_____

Mix ingredients all together and make patties; in large skillet add cooking oil and fry over medium heat until cooked thoroughly or you can throw them on the grill. Top with mayo, lettuce, maters, and onions for a great gobble burger.

MAW-MAW'S MAC-N-CHEESE

$\frac{1}{4}$ Cup of butter or margarine - divided
$\frac{1}{4}$ cup of flour
1 cup of milk
8 oz. of Velveeta Cheese- cut into $\frac{1}{2}$ inch cubes
2 cups of Elbow Macaroni -cooked
$\frac{1}{2}$ cup of shredded Cheddar Cheese
6 Ritz Crackers- crushed as crumbs

_____Mac Your Cheese in the Mouth_____

MELT 3 Tbsp. butter in medium saucepan on medium heat. Whisk in flour; cook 2 min., stirring constantly. Gradually stir in milk. Bring to boil; cook and stir 3 to 5 min. or until thickened. Add VELVEETA; cook 3 min. or until melted, stirring frequently. Stir in macaroni.

SPOON into 2-qt. casserole sprayed with cooking spray; sprinkle with cheddar. Melt remaining butter; toss with cracker crumbs. Sprinkle over casserole. BAKE 20 minutes at 350 degrees

Hot Hillbilly Party Dip

1 lb. Hot Pork Sausage

1 lb. Hamburger Meat

1 medium onion- chopped

2 lb of Velveeta Cheese

1 large jalapeno pepper- seeded and chopped

Milk

_____Get this hot party started!_____

Brown sausage, hamburger meat, and onions; Drain- Melt cheese in double broiler or microwave. Mix ingredients together adding milk to desired consistency.

Quit Trippin and Start Dippin'!

HILLBILLY YARD BIRD AND DUMPLINS

Chicken & Dumpling Casserole
2 lbs. of Yard Bird (Chicken thighs)...or you can use squirrel or possum for a true hillbilly cookin' experience.
1 C. all purpose flour
1 C. milk
2 T. unsalted butter, melted.
1-10oz can of cream of chicken soup
2 cups of chicken broth (Hillbilly tip- use the water you cooked the chicken in)
$\frac{1}{4}$ tsp of salt
$\frac{1}{2}$ tsp of black pepper

_____Grab your yard bird, possum, or squirrel_____

Place yard bird in a big pot and cover with water/ cover and cook over medium heat for 1 hour. Remove chicken from pot (save the water for chicken broth) and let cool. Shred chicken and place in the bottom of a 11x7 baking dish. Whisk together the flour, milk, and butter and pour over the chicken. Whisk together the broth, soup, salt and pepper, pour over the casserole (DO NOT STIR) Bake at 350 degrees for 45-50 minutes....Let it set for a few minutes before serving.

Hillbilly Weenie Chili

1 can of maters

1 can of kidney beans

1 lb of your favorite weenies

1 medium onion, chopped

¼ tsp chili powder

½ tsp salt

_____Grab yo' weenies and come on…_____
Cut them weenies up into small chunks. Mix all
ingredients and cook on medium heat for about 20
minutes or until onions are tender…

(Add cornbread or crackers to make it a Oh, this is a hillbilly good meal)

I'd say that's easy for any hillbilly to slang together for a quick meal…Hee Haw!

Hillbilly Veggie Soup

1 (12 oz) can of V-8 Juice (mild or spicy)

1 can of whole kernel corn

1 can of green beans

1 can of lima beans

1 can of sliced carrots (or fresh sliced carrots)

2 stalks of celery- chopped

$\frac{1}{2}$ onions- chopped

1 cup of water

Salt & pepper to taste

_____Havin' a veggie baptizing_____

Here come the Hillbilly rocket science way of cookin' this soup...get ya big pot, dump all the ingredients in and simmer fer 1 hour. If ya like a little kick in the seat of your soup, use the spicy V-8 mater juice. Wee Dawgie!

Grab ya fist full of cornbread and chow down!

Hillbilly Twangy Cole Slaw

1 Large head of cabbage

1 Cup dill pickles- chopped

1 Cup of Mayo

$\frac{3}{4}$ Cup of onions-chopped

2 Tbs. of prepared mustard

1 tsp of sugar

1 tsp celery seed

2 tsp of vinegar

Dash of salt & black pepper

_____Twang dat slaw_____

Shred enough cabbage to make 12 cups. Combine the cabbage, pickles, and onions in a large bowl; set it aside. Then mix together the mayo and remaining ingredients in a small bowl, salt & pepper and stir it well. Pour over cabbage mixture and toss it around. Cover and chill in the refrigerator before serving.

Slap dat on your next Hillbilly Hotdawg!

Hillbilly Tater Tacos

1 lb hamburger meat

4-6 baked taters (a good bakin' tater)

1 cup of Mexican blend cheese (or Sharp Cheddar)

1 pack of taco seasoning

1 cup of green onions- chopped

½ cup of jalapeno peppers- seeded and chopped

Salsa

Sour Cream

_____Talkin' Tater Tacos, Y'all_____

Brown hamburger meat and drain. Add the taco seasoning and water in according to the package directions. While baked taters are hot & ready, cut a large slit on the top of tater to open up and fluff for the taco meat, cheese, salsa, jalapenos, and sour cream to go on top of your hot tater.

Caution! You have a loaded baked tater in your hand!

Ocean Mountain Oyster Stew

1 large can of smoked oysters or two small cans

5 oyster cans of water

1 small finely diced onion

1 can of evaporated milk

1 stick of butter

Salt & pepper to taste

_____Hope ya find a pearl in this oyster stew_____

Put oysters, onions, water and butter in a large sauce pan. Bring to a boil and add milk and seasoning. Heat to boiling temperature again...Remove from heat and serve with oyster crackers or some good cracklin' cornbread.

HILLBILLY TATER SOUP

2 ½ lbs. of Baby Red Taters-Diced in small bite size

½ regular package of uncooked bacon-finely diced

1 medium onion (yellow) diced

¼ bunch of celery diced

8 cups of milk

4 cups of water

4 chicken bullions- use one of the cups of water (hot) to dissolve bullions

1 tsp. salt

¾ cup of flour

parsley

1 cup of whipping cream

Shredded Cheese- Cheddar or blend-Fried Bacon Bits-Chopped

1 tsp. pepper

¼ bunch of fresh chopped

green onions

_____It's Tater Time! _____

DIRECTIONS: Large Pot, boil potatoes in water-10 min. Drain and set aside -In sauté pan cook bacon until crisp-drain put bacon on paper towel to drain more. Add onions and celery to bacon sauté pan over med-high heat cook until celery and onions are tender-about 5 minutes

To the large Potato pot, add milk, water, bullion, salt and pepper-cook over med-high heat until mixture is very hot- about 8 minutes-DO NOT BOIL

In a small pan melt butter and add flour-mix well and cook over low-med heat until mixture bubbles, stirring 2-3 minutes to make roux

While constantly stirring soup and the roux slowly until soup is thick and creamy – about 4 minutes –Stir in parsley and whipped cream _Garnish with bacon bits and onions (serve hot)_

Hillbilly Tater Salad

4 cups of cubed, cooked Taters (4-6 medium)

1 cup of Mayo

2 Tbs. vinegar

1 tsp sugar

1 tsp salt

$\frac{1}{4}$ tsp black pepper

1 cup of diced celery

$\frac{1}{2}$ cup of onion – chopped

2 hard boiled eggs-chopped

_____Skin them Taters_____

Combine the first 6 ingredients, stir in the remaining ingredients… cover and Chill. Yields= 5-6 servings.

Hillbilly Stuffed Jalapeno Oinkers

Wanna make your whistle tingle? This will make you squeal like a pig! Wee Doggie!

8oz. of cream cheese / or you can use cheddar cheese

$\frac{1}{4}$ cup of diced green onion (Hillbilly breath freshener)

$\frac{1}{2}$ cup of cooked and crumbled BACON (Dat's the oinker)

$\frac{1}{2}$ tsp of garlic salt

$\frac{1}{2}$ tsp of salt

$\frac{1}{2}$ tsp. of black pepper

$\frac{1}{2}$ tsp. Cajun seasoning

6 Large Jalapenos- Split

_____Oink, Oink said the Bacon_____

Split jalapenos and remove seeds and membranes (Hillbilly term- just gut them suckers) Soften cheese and mix all the other ingredients together and stuff all the goodies inside the split jalapenos and slap them babies on the grill for 20-25 minutes, top off the grilled jalapenos with some of the crumbled cooked bacon...grab you something cold to drink and enjoy!

Hillbilly South of the Hills Mac-n-Cheese

1 (8 oz) box of Mexican Velveeta cheese-cubed

1 (8 oz) Box of large elbow macaroni shells

$\frac{1}{2}$ cup of chunky salsa

1 tsp of taco seasoning

$\frac{1}{4}$ cup of green onions- chopped

1 jalapeno pepper- seeded and chopped finely

_____Set dat Mac-n-Cheese on fire!_____

Cook the macaroni as directed on box; drain. Mix macaroni with cheese and taco seasoning. Stir in the salsa and top with the green onions. Pour into a greased casserole dish and bake at 350 degrees for 20-25 minutes.

Dat's the Hillbilly Mac Daddy!

Hillbilly Sloppy Joes

1 lb. Hamburger Meat

4-6 Weenies - cut into small chunks

½ cup of onion bits

1 cup of BBQ Sauce

¼ cup of pickle relish

Cheese spread

8 count Hamburger Buns

_____Let's Get Sloppy Hillbilly Style_____

Brown the Hamburger meat and drain. Add weenie chunks, BBQ sauce, onion bits, and pickle relish. Cover and simmer for 15 minutes. Spread the cheese spread on the bottom half of the bun first...then top with meat mixture. Makes 8 sandwiches.

Hillbilly Made Easy Chicken-n- Dumplins

4 skinless, boneless chicken breast halves

2 Tbs. butter

2 cans of condensed cream of chicken soup

1 yellow onion- finely diced

2 (10 count) cans of biscuits- cut into small dumplin' size
pieces

_____Makin' Dumplins the Easy Way_____

Place chicken, soup, onions, and butter in a crock pot and
fill with enough water to cover it all up.

Cover the pot and cook for 5-6 hours on high. 25-30
minutes before serving it, place the biscuit dough in the
crock pot... Cook until dough is no longer raw. Hee Haw,
Y'all!

HILLBILLY LIAR'S CRAB CAKES

Veggie Oil for frying

2 (6 oz.) cans of tuna fish

1 egg, beaten

2 Tbs. diced green onions

$\frac{1}{4}$ cup of Mayo

$\frac{1}{2}$ cup bread crumbs

$\frac{1}{2}$ Tbs. Lemon juice is optional

_____ Liar, Liar, Britches on fire_____

Heat 1-inch of oil in a large skillet over medium heat-
While oil is heating, combine tuna, beaten egg, green
onions, mayo, $\frac{1}{4}$ cup of bread crumbs and lemon juice if
used- Form into patties and dust with additional bread
crumbs- When oil is hot, fry patties until golden brown
(about 2 minutes on each side) Remove from oil and drain
on paper towel before serving.

Hillbilly Jambalaya

1 cup of cooked chicken-chopped

1 cup of ham- chopped

10 pork sausage links-chopped

1 cup onions-chopped

1 cup of green bell pepper-chopped

2 cloves of garlic- chopped

2 Tbs. of canola or olive oil

1 large can of maters

1 cup of rice

1 tsp parsley

1 tsp salt

2 ½ cups of chicken broth

Black Pepper and Cajun seasoning to taste

_____Wee Doggie, Bring out the Hillbilly Cajun in ya!_____
Sauté onion, bell pepper and garlic in oil; add chicken, ham, and sausage; cook 5 minutes-Add in remaining ingredients & meat mixture and put into a large casserole dish. Bake at 350 degrees for 1 hour.

Hillbilly Joe's Sloppy Jalapeno Burger

2 lb. Hamburger Meat

¼ cup of ketchup

1 pack of sloppy Joe seasoning mix

American or Pepper Jack single slices of Cheese

Large jalapeno pepper- seeded and finely chopped

8 Hamburger buns

_____Get Sloppy with Hillbilly Joe_____

Mix all the ingredients together- hamburger meat, ketchup, jalapenos, and sloppy Joe mix and make them in to some great lookin' patties. In a large fryin' pan fry them until meat is cooked all the way done. You can also grill these babies up. Slap the cheese on top of the burger just before pulling them from cooking to let the cheese get a good melt down. Pull out dat bun and slap a sloppy burger on it and top with your favorite toppings and chow down!

There's no Hillbilly law that keeps ya from getting sloppy

Hillbilly Pizzer Samwiches

2 lb hamburger meat

2 cups of pepperonis- chopped

1 (15oz) jar or can of pizza sauce

1 cup chopped bell pepper

1 cup of onions- chopped

1 cup of black olives- sliced

1 can of Rotel tomatoes (mild)

1 bag of Pizza blend shredded cheese

12 English Muffins

_____This is not delivery, its home made_____

Bring out a large skillet and cook the hamburger meat, onions and bell peppers over medium heat until meat is totally cooked; drain. Stir in the olives, pepperonis, pizza sauce and tomatoes, and continue to simmer for 5-6 minutes; stir occasionally. Toast the English Muffins and top with the mixture on each muffin half and sprinkle with the cheese.

Country Mama's Coleslaw

6 cups cabbage, shredded (can use a bag of coleslaw mix from the produce section)

1 red apple, unpeeled and diced small (optional)

1/2 cup carrot, shredded

1/4 cup sweet onion, chopped fine

Dressing

1/2 cup sugar

1/2 cup water

1/4 cup vinegar (apple cider vinegar or white vinegar either one works)

1 cup mayonnaise

2 tsp. honey mustard (prepared dressing or just the prepared honey mustard dipping sauce or sandwich spread)

1 tsp. prepared yellow mustard

_____Get out your Granny's Big Bowl_____

Mix cabbage, apple, carrot and onion in a large mixing bowl. The apple is optional, but I would advise trying it, it makes the coleslaw so much better. Dice the apple into a bowl of salted, warm water first and let it sit for a minute or two, then drain. This keeps it from turning brown and the slaw can be kept for two to three days in the refrigerator if you have leftovers.

For the dressing, combine the sugar, water and vinegar and microwave for about 3 minutes or cook over medium heat in a saucepan until it comes to a boil and boil for a minute or two. Set aside and cool completely. You can place it in the refrigerator to cool it faster.

Once cool, stir in the mayonnaise, the honey mustard, and the yellow mustard. Pour the dressing mixture over the shredded cabbage and other ingredients and mix well. This is best if you refrigerate for at least 2 hours for the flavors to blend. Stir again right before serving.

HILLBILLY HOTDAWGS

Every Hillbilly loves hotdawgs (hotdogs). It's one of the favorite foods of a true hillbilly. It's a simple meal that brings enjoyment to all. There are so many ways to dress up your Dawgs. Hillbilly Dave knows good hotdawgs when he taste one and I want to share some of my ideas to make your next dawg a great one! We hillbillies love our dawgs like no other ones across the nation does, cause we love 'em with mustard, chili, slaw, and onions...Wee dawggy!

_____THE HILLBILLY DAWG_____

8 count pack of your favorite jumbo weenies

Mustard

Chili (recipe on next page 77)

Cole Slaw- you can make your own or buy it

White onions

8 count pack of hotdawg buns

Slap that fat weenie on a bun put on the mustard, add they chili, and top it off with cole slaw and onions....now you're eatin' a dawg hillbilly style.

HILLBILLY HOTDAWG CHILI RECIPE

There is no store bought canned chili or as some call it, hotdog sauce that makes the cut...they all taste like, well, you know...so here's a recipe that will dress up your dawg and make it taste great!

_____Ingredients to a great Chili (Sauce)_____

1 lb. ground beef

1 (6 oz.) can of tomato paste

1 cup of water

¼ tsp of red pepper- crushed (more or less- how much you love the heat?)

1 tsp of onion powder

1 tsp of salt

1 tsp of black pepper

1 tsp. of minced garlic

2 Tbs. chili powder

_____Top your dawg with this_____

In a large skillet put in ground beef (Don't brown meat first) Add water, (Don't add too much water it will make the chili too soupy) add the rest of the ingredients, stir well -cook on medium-high heat making sure to chop up the ground beef while cooking to small pieces...once it starts to boil, reduce heat and simmer for 45 minutes. Top dat dawg off with that!

THE PIZZERIA DAWG

Get your pizza and eat your dog all at the same time...

8 Count pack of your favorite weenies

Pizza Sauce

Mozzarella Cheese - Shredded

Pepperonis

White onions- Diced up

8 count pack of your favorite hotdawg buns

_____Dat Puppy Will Hunt_____

Put your favorite weenie on a bun, pour pizza sauce across the weenie, put the cheese across the dawg, cut your pepperoni slices in half (4-6 half pieces per dawg) sauté them in a skillet to get them good and warm, put them on top of the cheese and sprinkle with white onions...you can put the dawgs under the broiler for a few seconds to melt the cheese. Enjoy!

KIDS LOVE THEM PIZZER DAWGS!

Hillbilly Hamburger Weenie Dawg

1 lb. Hamburger Meat

½ cup of pickle relish

½ cup of BBQ sauce

2 Tbs. Minced Onion

Salt & Pepper to taste

White onion- Chopped

Hotdog Chili (see recipe)

Cole Slaw

Mustard

Hotdog buns

_____Who let this dawgs out?_____

Combine the hamburger meat, relish, BBQ sauce, and minced onion, salt & pepper to taste and shape in the form of a hotdawg weenie and brown it in a skillet turning it several times to cook evenly; Cook about 5-6 minutes - Place in a nice steamed bun and top with Mustard, Chili, Slaw, and white onions.

HILLBILLY STEAK DAWG

8 count pack of your favorite weenies

Slices of Swiss cheese (slices like American cheese)

Bold flavored Steak Sauce (your choice)

1 large green bell pepper (cut in strips)

1 Large white onion (cut in strips)

2 Tbs. Olive Oil (to sauté)

Celery salt

8 count pack of buns

_____Make those weenies taste like T-Bones_____

Put the weenie on a hot steamed bun, cut Swiss Cheese into 1inch strips and place two pieces on the weenie, pour bold steak sauce across the dawg, sauté bell pepper & onions in Olive Oil and put on top and sprinkle with the celery salt...

Hillbilly-Mexican Dawg

8 count of your favorite jumbo weenies

Salsa

Corn Chips

Mexican blend shredded cheese

Jalapenos- sliced

8 count hotdog buns

_____Make your dawg talk Taco_____

Place a jumbo weenie on a hot steamed bun, pour salsa across the weenie, put corn chips on next, load on the Mexican cheese, and top off with jalapenos. Put it in the over under "broil" for a minute to melt the cheese. If you want you can put a dab of sour cream on top after you melt the cheese.

Listen! I hear my dawg barkin' Spanish

Hillbilly Chili Cheese Jalapeno Dawg

8 count of your favorite jumbo weenies

1 can of Nacho Cheese Sauce (warmed)

Chili (see recipe)

Sliced jalapenos

8 count hotdog buns

_____Cheese up my Dawg!_____

Put a jumbo weenie on your steamed hot bun, the pour the Nacho cheese sauce across the weenie, add the chili and top it off with the jalapeno slices.

That'll make your jalapeno bark!

HILLBILLY HUNTIN' GRUB

Hunting is a way of life in the Appalachian Mountains.
Hillbillies learn to hunt at a very young age. We are not
only out there to see how big of a deer, bear, possum,
snake, or squirrel we can get; we help feed a hungry
family with the blessings from the woods.

   I'm not going to leave our fellow hunters out of this
great cookbook, so we've put in some wild game recipes for
the entire family to enjoy!

_____Happy Hillbilly Huntin', Y'all!_____

Hillbilly Dave

Mountain Man's Deer Roast

1 (3-4 lb) Deer Roast

Pepper it to your taste

1 pack of onion soup mix

1 envelope of hamburger seasoning

1 garlic clove chopped, or use garlic salt to taste

1 can cream of celery soup

2 cups water

_____Roast that baby up!_____

Season the roast to taste with pepper. Sprinkle soup mix over roast, then add hamburger seasoning and garlic over roast. Spread the celery soup over roast; add water and cover and cook at 250 degrees for 2- 2 $\frac{1}{2}$ hours. Add more water if needed. Yields= 8 -10 servings.

Hillbilly Country-Fried Deer Steak

2 lb. of deer steak

1 cup self-rising flour

½ cup of vinegar

1 cup water

½ cup milk

1 egg

1 Tbs. Salt

Pepper to taste

Garlic salt to taste

Fryin' Oil- Veggie, Canola, or Peanut Oil

_____How do ya like your steak?_____

Pound steak until tender- Soak steak in vinegar, water, and salt for 1 hour to draw out blood and wild gamy taste. Remove from brine and dry with paper towels. In a bowl mix milk and egg to make a egg & milk wash. Dip in wash then roll in flour, black pepper, and garlic salt. Fry in a large deep sided skillet in oil over medium heat until done.

Dat's what hillbillies call country fried deer steak!

Hillbilly Baked Whistle Pig

1 groundhog (Whistle Pig)

2 Tbs. salt

1 medium onion- Chopped

1tsp black pepper

1 pod of red pepper

_____Whistle While You Cook_____

Place whole groundhog in a large kettle; cover with water then add the salt, onions, and red pepper; boil for 3 hours until dat groundhog is tender. Remove from water; place on a baking sheet. Sprinkle with black pepper. Bake at 450 degrees for 20 minutes or until the top of it is brown.

Best Whistle Pig in the pot...Enjoy!

Hillbilly Gone Nuts Baked Squirrel

4 squirrels- cleaned and dressed

1 can of bouillon

¼ cup Worcestershire Sauce

2 Tbs. parsley- chopped

2 Tbs. onion juice

1 clove of garlic- minced

1 small bay leaf

Flour for squirrel

Salt, seasoning salt, and pepper to your taste buds

_____YOU"LL GO NUTS OVER THIS!_____

Flour squirrel and brown in roasting pan. Add all the other ingredients and bake at 350 degrees for 45 minutes. Reduce heat and bake slowly for another 45 min. or until tender….Yield = 4 servings.

Country Fried Rattlesnake

Make sure to cut off the rattlers and make a Hillbilly toy for your baby

1 large Rattle snake- gutted and skinned

Salt & Pepper

1 quart of peanut oil (for fryin' dat snake)

2 chicken eggs- beaten well

$\frac{1}{4}$ cup of milk

Flour

_____Shake, Rattle, and Roll_____

Cut dat snake up into chunk pieces; salt & pepper that rascal. Make the batter of milk and eggs. Dip the snake in the batter then roll into the flour. Fry in hot peanut oil until golden brown. Serve Hot!

Servings depend on how big of a rattler you got.

Big Rack Deer Loaf

2 ½ lbs of deer burger

1 lb pork sausage

2 eggs

2 tsp salt

1 tsp pepper

2 small onions-chopped

4 Tbsp Worcestershire Sauce

1 ½ cups of bread crumbs

_____Look at the rack on dat loaf_____

Soak the bread crumbs in some stock. Mix all ingredients and shape into a loaf and put in a loaf pan. Bake at 400 degrees for 1 hour.

Dawg-Gone Good Deer Stew

2 lb of deer stew meat

1 red bell pepper-slice in strips

1 large onion -chopped

1 tsp salt

3 Tbs. of bacon drippings or Veggie Oil

2 Tbs. flour

1 pint of mater juice

1 Tbs. Worcestershire Sauce

_____Get your deer all stewed up!_____

In a large deep skillet...Stew meat with peppers until it slips from the bone or its tender. Add onion and salt- continue to cook. In separate pan, heat oil or bacon drippings and add flour and stir constantly until brown. Add mater sauce and Worcestershire sauce. Add this gravy stew and continue to cook for 1 hour. 8 Servings

Paw's Sawmill Biscuit Gravy

1 lb of your favorite pork sausage (Mild or Spicy)

2-3 Tbs. flour

1 $\frac{1}{2}$ cups of milk

$\frac{1}{2}$ tsp salt

$\frac{1}{2}$ pepper

Cathead Biscuits

_____Sawin' some gravy for dah biscuits_____

Cook sausage in fryin' pan and crumble it up. Remove sausage and set aside. Keep grease from cooked sausage to make the gravy. Brown flour in hot grease, stirring it constantly. Add milk gradually to desired thickness. Return Sausage to gravy. Add in the salt & pepper.

Pour over your cathead biscuits and saw away!

Hillbilly Jalapeno Cornbread Puddin'

4 cups of cornbread (crumbled)

4 eggs (lightly beaten)

2 cups of heavy whipping cream

1 ½ cups of whole kernel corn

½ yellow onion (diced)

1 Tbsp canola or veggie oil

2 cups of pepper jack cheese (shredded) Divide 2 cups

Salt & Pepper to taste

1 large jalapeno pepper (seeded and sliced thin rings)

2 large red or green bell peppers (seeded and sliced thin)

_____Dat'll make your whistler tingle_____

Preheat oven to 350 degrees. Grease an 8" pan. Heat oil in a large skillet and sauté onions until tender; remove from heat and stir in eggs, cream, cornbread and 1 cup of cheese and season with salt and pepper: pour mixture in the greased pan and sprinkle with the other cup of cheese and place the rings of jalapenos and bell peppers on top. Place pan in a water bath and bake for 1 hour.

Hillbilly Apple Butter

4 cups of apples

3 cups of sugar

1 tsp. cinnamon

1 package of strawberry Jello

_____Slap dat butter on some cathead biscuits_____

Cook the apples in a large pot, and mash the devil out of them until they are mashed fine; add the sugar and cinnamon and cook until thick. Add the box of jello mix and cook for 5 more minutes.

Hillbilly Crazy Butter

2 sticks of butter at room temperature

1 cup of powder sugar

1 cup of honey

2 tsp of ground cinnamon

_____Butter it up and make it go crazy!_____
Mix it all together until you get the right consistency. Get ya some little jars and load them full of butter and put in the frigerator. This butter will be great on hot rolls, toast, pancakes, waffles, or anything that needs good butter.

Hillbilly Butter is better than all the other...Hee Haw!

Hillbilly Bread Section

The Good Book says a man can't live by bread alone, but sometimes you think that we hillbillies are trying to do just that with all the good types of breads out there...This old hillbilly loves his bread and I hope you do too...Here's some recipes that will dress up a table full of great bread and make your taste buds holler for more. Enjoy!

Happy Eatin'

Hillbilly Dave

Sweet Tater Biscuits

1 Cup of cooked, mashed fresh sweet taters

Quick Fix: you can use canned sweet taters (15 oz. can)

4 cups biscuit mix

$\frac{1}{2}$ tsp cinnamon

$\frac{3}{4}$ cup of milk

3 Tbs. butter / softened

_____Maw, there's a sweet tater in my biscuit_____
Preheat oven to 450 degrees. In a bowl, mix sweet taters, biscuit mix and cinnamon; add milk and butter and stir until well blended. Roll onto a floured surface to 1 inch thick; cut with a two inch cutter or glass and place on ungreased baking sheet. Bake 10-12 minutes or until them suckers are golden brown. Hee Haw, Y'all!

Paw's Mother-n-Law's Bread

3 qt. sifted flour

2 cups of scaled milk

$\frac{1}{4}$ cup sugar

1 $\frac{1}{2}$ Tbsp salt

3 Tbsp of canola or veggie oil

3 cups of warm water

1 package of dry yeast-dissolved in $\frac{1}{4}$ cup of warm water

__Butter up the Mother-n-Law when the bread is done__
Place the flour in a large bowl; mix milk, sugar, salt, oil, and water; Make a well in the flour; pour in the milk mixture and mix in flour gradually; add the yeast and mix very well. Knead on a flour coated surface and place in a bowl and let rise until double in size. Shape into 3 loaves Place in 3 bread loaf pans and bake at 350 degrees for 30 minutes. Goes great with Hillbilly Butter (see recipe in cookbook) Yummy fo' da Tummy!

Hillbilly Jalapeno Hush Puppies

1 ½ cups of cornmeal

½ cup of flour

2 Tbsp of baking powder

2 Tbsp of sugar

½ tsp of salt

2 eggs

Milk

1 small onion finely chopped

1 jalapeno pepper- seeded and finely chopped

Canola or Veggie Oil for deep frying

_____Hush them puppies up_____

Combine cornmeal, flour, baking powder, sugar and salt. Mix eggs and enough milk to make soft dough. Add to dry mixture; stir in onions and jalapenos. Drop from teaspoon into oil; cook for about 3 minutes or until brown. Drain on paper towel. Serve 'em with some country fried catfish.

Hillbilly Raisin Cornbread

1 ¼ cup of flour

¾ cup of cornmeal

½ cup raisins

Sugar

3 ½ tsp of baking powder

Cinnamon

2 Tbs. veggie or canola oil

¼ tsp allspice

¼ tsp ginger

1 Tbs. butter

¾ tsp salt

1 cup milk

1 egg-slightly beaten

_____Raisin Cane on Some Cornbread!_____

Sift flour, ¼ cup sugar, baking powder, 1 tsp cinnamon, salt, ginger, allspice and cornmeal together. Combine egg, milk, oil and raisins; add to dry ingredients. Mix until batter is smooth. Put it into a well greased 11x7 inch or 9x9 inch pan. Cut butter, ½ cup of sugar, and 1 tsp cinnamon together until fine. Spread over batter. Bake at 400 degrees for 25 minutes. Cool before serving.

Hillbilly Sausage Made Cornbread

½ lb of your favorite pork sausage (hot or mild)

1 (14 oz.) pack of corn muffin or corn bread mix

2 eggs

¼ cup of milk

1 regular can of cream style corn

_____Pig up your cornbread_____

Preheat oven to 400 degrees. In a large bowl, mix together eggs, milk, and corn. Stir in cornbread mix until blended. Fold in sausage (want a hillbilly kick, add spicy hot sausage). Pour cornbread mix into a grease iron skillet or pan. Bake for 20-25 minutes until golden brown.

Taste the oink in dat cornbread!

CABIN FEVER FRENCH TOAST

½ Cup of melted butter (1 stick)

1 cup of brown sugar

1 loaf of Texas Toast

4 eggs

1 ½ cups of milk

1tsp. of Vanilla

Powder Sugar for sprinkling on top of toast

_____No Toaster Needed Here!_____

1. Melt butter in microwave and add brown sugar (mix well)
2. Pour butter/sugar mix into the bottom of 9x13 pan (spread it)
3. Beat eggs, milk, and vanilla
4. Lay a single layer of Texas Toast in pan
5. Spoon ½ of egg mixture on bread layer
6. Add second layer of Texas Toast
7. Spoon remainder of egg mixture on 2nd layer of toast
8. Cover & Chill overnight
9. Bake @ 350 degrees for 45 minutes (Cover for the first 30 min.)

Sprinkle with powdered sugar and serve with warm maple syrup.

MEX-A-BILLY CORNBREAD

Mix in a little Mexican & Hillbilly and you got some great cornbread!

2 cups of cornmeal

2 Tbsp flour

1 Tbsp baking powder

½ tsp salt

1 cup of milk (Buttermilk is optional)

1 small onion- chopped

2 eggs

1 can of whole kernel corn

1 cup of cheddar cheese, grated

3 jalapeno peppers- chopped

½ cup of cooking oil

½ tsp of baking soda

_____Mex-A-Billy Your Bread_____

Mix dry ingredients; stir in milk, eggs, and oil- Add other ingredients and bake in greased iron skillet for 30 minutes at 350 degrees...Makes a hillbilly want to do the Cha-Cha.

HILLBILLY DROP KICK BISCUITS

2 cups of flour

1 stick of butter

1 Tbs. baking powder

1 tsp of salt

$\frac{1}{2}$ tsp of baking soda

$\frac{1}{2}$ cream of tartar

4 Tbs. shortening

1 cup of buttermilk

_____Drop Kick the Dough_____

Sift dry ingredients together x two- using two knives, cut shortening into flour mixture until it's well mixed. Add the buttermilk-stir until well! Drop level Tablespoons of dough onto a greased   cookie sheet. Place a pat of butter on each biscuit Preheat oven to 450 degrees and bake biscuits for 10-12 minutes or until golden brown. This should make around 25 biscuits and taste so good that you will want to drop kick your granny.

HILLBILLY FRIED CORNBREAD

<u>Ingredients:</u>
1 egg
1 cup self rising flour
1 cup self rising corn meal
1 cup milk or buttermilk
1 Tbs. sugar
1/2 Tbs. baking powder (you can leave this out, but it makes the hoe cakes rise up really nice)

_____ YOU GOT A LOT TO DO SO START MIXIN'_____

Start by mixing together an egg, 1 cup self rising flour, 1 cup self rising corn meal, 1 cup milk or buttermilk, 1 Tbs sugar, and 1/2 Tbs baking powder. If you use buttermilk, you might need to add 1/4 cup water because it makes it a little thicker. Mix all ingredients

Heat vegetable oil in a skillet just to coat it on medium high heat. When you pour batter in it should sizzle, but no smoke. You can use a nonstick skillet or an iron skillet or a griddle if you have one.

Do not flip until they start to bubble and get little craters in them, then you can turn them without them falling apart. They are pretty much done now and just need to brown on the other side.

Cook on the other side for about 3-5 minutes or until brown and you have delicious hoe cakes. Here is a helpful tip, do not be tempted to press down on these once you flip them. They are not hamburgers and pressing on them will make them tough and dense not light

***If you cannot buy self rising cornmeal and self rising flour in your area, use all purpose and add tsp. baking powder, 1 tsp. baking soda, and 1/4 tsp. salt. If you can buy self rising, invest in some, it just makes better cornbread.

Hillbilly Cat Head Biscuits

Make 'em as big as your cat's head....now dat's hillbilly big!

1 Cup of Sifted Self-Rising Flour
2 tbsp. of shortening
1/3 cups of milk
Pinch of salt

_____Make them biscuits meow_____

Preheat oven to 475 degrees. Cut shortening into flour with a pinch of salt using your mixer to blend it all together until particles are fine. Add milk and stir until dough clings together. Knead lightly on flour coated board or pastry cloth. Roll out to desire thickness...using a flour coated cutter, cut them suckers as big as a cat's head and place them on an ungreased baking sheet and pop them in the oven for 8-10 minutes....

Bring out the apple butter and get dat cat scratch fever working...

Crazy Country Cheese Biscuits

2 cups of flour

1 stick of butter

1 tsp. baking powder

2 cups of grated cheddar cheese (mild or sharp)

$\frac{1}{4}$ tsp. salt

Dash of crushed red pepper

_____Get Cheesy With Them Crazy Biscuits_____

Mix all the ingredients until smooth; chill. Slice about $\frac{1}{4}$ inch thick; place on a cookie sheet and bake at 375 degrees for 15 minutes or until golden brown. Don't overcook 'em...

Best thang since sliced bread!

BREAKFAST TIME CORN CAKES

2 cups of buttermilk

$\frac{1}{4}$ tsp. of flour

$\frac{1}{4}$ tsp of baking soda

2 tsp baking powder

1 cup of corn meal

1 egg

$\frac{1}{2}$ tsp of salt

1 tsp of sugar

_____Grab the corn by the ears!_____

Mix all the ingredients, using more corn meal if needed and add the baking powder last. Do not beat the batter cause it's better if it sits awhile. Cook like pancakes on a greased griddle or in a fryin' pan.

Replace them cathead biscuits with these cakes and eat them with bacon and eggs!

Country Boy Corn Bread Dressing

4 cups of pork or chicken stock

3 eggs-slightly beaten

2 cups of crumbled cornbread

1 ½ cups of dry bread crumbs

½ cup of melted butter

1/3 cup of onion-finely diced

1/8 tsp black pepper

1 tsp salt

_____Stuff this up your Bird_____

Combine all ingredients and mix well. Bake for 30 minutes at 450 degrees. Yield= enough dressing for a 4 Lb chicken. If you would like to stuff a turkey, just double the amount of ingredients for a double batch of the best dressing around. Get dressed and come on to the table.

Billy Bob's Bacon Corn Muffins

1 lb. Bacon (Hickory or Apple-wood smoked)

1 cup of cornmeal

½ cup of self-rising flour

1 tsp sugar

1 egg

1 ½ cups of milk

_____Listen to the Oink in these Muffins_____

Sift cornmeal, flour, salt, and sugar together. Fry bacon until crisp; crumble bacon into medium size pieces. Add to dry ingredients. Add egg to milk; beat well. Stir into dry mixture, mixing until blended well. Spoon batter into muffin pans; Bake at 450 degrees for 15 minutes

Casseroles

Growing up in the Appalachian Mountains as a kid, I was fascinated by the 7 wonders of the world, and I thought being a Hillbilly was one of the seven wonders; but I just had to add one more to the line up and make the Casserole the 8th wonder of the world to make things complete. Casseroles have fed Hillbilly families for many years. They are easy to make, easy to bake, and fun to eat. All you have to do is gather ingredients from the kitchen throw them in a greased casserole dish, bake and enjoy the best grub that money can buy. So I have decided to add a special section to this Hillbilly Cookbook for you and your family to enjoy. So get out your casserole dish and make it a Hillbilly Hoe Down...It's chow time!

Happy Eatin' Y'all

Hillbilly Dave

Uncle Shorty's Short Rib Casserole

3 lb. of beef short ribs

3 medium onions, chopped

2 cans of tomatoes

1 large carrot, sliced

½ cup of rice

¼ tsp. pepper

1 ½ tsp. salt

1 tsp. sugar

_____There's nuttin short about my ribs_____

In a large skillet use 3 Tbsp. of cooking oil; add onions and ribs and brown well. Place in casserole dish. Combine tomatoes, carrot, rice and seasonings; pour over ribs and onions. Add enough hot water to cover ingredients; cover and bake at 350 degrees for about 3 hours. Add additional water if needed. This will feed 8 hungry hillbillies.

Garden fresh veggies casserole

2 large onions cut in ½ inch slices

4 large firm tomatoes cut in ½ inch slices

2 cups of diced taters

1 cup of chopped celery

1 cup of sliced carrots

1 tsp. salt

¼ tsp. of black pepper

1 tsp. paprika

¼ cup of canola or veggie oil

_____Maw said you better eat yo' veggies_____

Layer onions, tomatoes, taters, celery and carrots in a greased casserole dish. Sprinkle each layer with salt, pepper and paprika; add the oil. Cover and bake at 375 degrees for 1 hour or until veggies are tender...this will feed 4-6 hungry hillbilly gardeners.

Uncle Salty's Sardine Casserole

Don't knock it until ya try it...

2 large cans of sardines (skinned and deboned)

1 can of cream of mushroom soup

4 cups of cooked sliced taters

1 small onion (chopped)

$\frac{1}{4}$ cup of chopped celery

2 Tbsp. of butter

8 pimento stuffed olives (sliced)

_____Let's go fishin' with Uncle Salty_____

Brown onions and celery in butter; add taters and soup.
Place half of the stanky little fish on the bottom of a
greased casserole dish; add soup & tater mixture. Put
remaining sardines on top. Garnish with the olives to make
dat fish look pretty. Cover it up and bake at 350 degrees
for 40 minutes. Dat fishy catch will feed about four of
Uncle Salty's friends.

Aunt Pearl's Oyster Casserole

1 pint of fresh oysters

1 can of chicken-gumbo soup

2 cups of cracker crumbs

4 tsp. melted butter

Salt & Pepper to taste

_____Oysters make Hillbillies love everybody_____

Make single layers of oysters, salt & pepper and cracker crumbs in a casserole dish and repeat the layers until all the of the ingredients are used. Pour butter on top. Cover it with the mushroom soup. Bake at 350 degrees until top is golden brown. Serve dat baby when it's hot!

If you find a pearl in your casserole, give me a call...

Hillbilly Mackerel Casserole

1 can of mackerel (drained and flaked)

1 can of cream of mushroom soup

2 eggs (slightly beaten)

1 tsp. dry mustard

$\frac{1}{2}$ tsp of salt and a dash of pepper

$\frac{1}{2}$ small onion (chopped)

3 slices of bread (cubed)

_____Holy Mackerel, I smell something fishy_____

Combine the eggs, seasonings, onion, bread and soup. Add the mackerel; mix very well. Place in a grease casserole dish. Bake at 375 degrees for 40 minutes. Feeds about 6 Hillbilly Mackerel Lovers...

Tater Chip & Tuna Casserole

1 can of tuna

1 can of cream of mushroom soup

1 cup of milk

1 cup of crushed tater chips

_____Tater up your Tuna_____

Combine tuna, soup and milk in a mixing bowl. Add $\frac{3}{4}$ cup of
crushed tater chips; mix well. Pour into a greased
casserole dish; sprinkle with remaining tater chips over
top. Bake at 375 degrees for 30 minutes. Feeds 4-6
Hungry Hillbillies

Best thang from dat fishin' hole-taters & tuna

HILLBILLY HOT-DAWG CASSEROLE

10 count weenies

7 oz. package elbow macaroni

1 cup shredded carrots

$\frac{1}{4}$ green bell pepper-chopped

$\frac{1}{2}$ tsp dill weed

$\frac{1}{2}$ cup onions-chopped

1 can cream celery soup

8 oz. sour cream

_____Weenie Up!_____

Cook macaroni and drain- Cut 6 weenies into little chunks, leaving 4 whole weenies. Spray casserole dish...Combine macaroni and remaining ingredients except whole weenies; bake uncovered at 350 degrees for 25 minutes. Slice the whole weenies in half (Long ways) and lay them on top of casserole and bake for 15 minutes more

Crawdaddy Creek Seafood Casserole

½ lb. crab meat

½ lb. cooked shrimp

½ lb. cooked crawfish tails

1 cup of mayo

1 ½ cup of chopped celery

½ cup of chopped onions

½ cup of chopped bell pepper

½ tsp. salt

1 tsp. Worcestershire sauce

1 cup of potato chips (crushed)

Paprika

_____Down at the crawfish hole without a pole_____

Combine all the ingredients except chips and paprika. Pour into a greased casserole dish. Cover with chips and sprinkle with paprika. Bake at 350 degrees for 30-40 minutes. Feeds 6 Crawdaddies and Crawmamas

Aunt Tiny's Meat & Tater Casserole

$\frac{1}{4}$ lb. of hamburger meat

$\frac{1}{4}$ lb. sausage (mild or hot)

5 medium taters (diced)

$\frac{1}{4}$ cup chopped onions

1 - Small can of tomato puree

$\frac{1}{2}$ bell pepper (seeded and sliced in thin rings)

1-2 large jalapeno pepper (seeded and cut into thin rings)

Salt & Pepper to taste

_____This casserole ain't Tiny on Taste_____

Combine all the ingredients except for the taters and bell pepper. Brown those taters in a small amount of cooking oil. Add to hamburger and sausage mixture. Place mixture in a casserole dish and place bell pepper and jalapenos on top. Bake at 350 degrees for 45 minutes. Feeds Aunt Tiny and five of her hillbilly friends...

Maw's Mac-N- Ham Casserole

8 oz. macaroni (cooked and drained)

2 cups of ham (diced in bite size pieces)

1 ½ cups of sharp grated cheddar cheese

2- 8oz. cans of tomato sauce

¼ cup of butter

1 tsp. of minced garlic

½ tsp. salt

¼ tsp. ground black pepper

_____Dat'll make you Mac yo' Hawg!_____

Melt butter in a sauce pan; add tomato sauce, onion, garlic, salt & pepper, simmer for 10 minutes. Add the ham and ¾ cup of cheese; heat til cheese melts and stir in macaroni. Pour into greased casserole dish; sprinkle with remaining cheese on top. Bake at 350 degrees for 30 minutes.

Dat'll feed 5 hungry hawgs! Hee Haw, Maw!

Wild Turkey Casserole

Now you know what to do with leftover turkey at Thanksgivin'

2 cups of Turkey - cooked & chopped

1 can of cream of chicken soup

2 tsp chopped onion

1 cup of chopped celery

½ tsp pepper

¼ tsp salt

1 cup slivered almonds

1 tsp lemon juice

½ cup of mayo

3 hard-boiled eggs-chopped

½ cup crushed tater chips

_____Grab Yo' Gobbler and Come On_____

Combine all ingredients except the tater chips; mix well. Pour into a casserole dish; sprinkle with tater chips. Bake at 375 degrees for 25 minutes. Gobble this up!

Fanny's Five Can Casserole

1 large can of canned chicken

1 can chicken with rice soup

1 can for mushroom soup

1 6 oz. can of evaporated milk

1 can of Chow Mein noodles

_____Dat ain't no fuzzy math...ya only need five_____

Mix all the ingredients together and place it in a casserole dish. Bake at 350 degrees for 45 minutes...Feeds 4 of Fanny's friends...Now ain't dat the easiest casserole you ever put together? Dat's what I thought.

Dat Five Deal Casserole goes great with biscuits!

Rowdy Rooster's Chicken Salad Casserole

1 large can of canned chicken

1 can of chicken soup

2 cups crushed tater chips

3 hard boiled eggs (sliced)

2 Tbsp of minced onion

1 cup of minced celery

$\frac{1}{2}$ of chopped walnuts

$\frac{3}{4}$ cup of mayo

$\frac{1}{2}$ tsp. of salt and pepper

_____Let's get rowdy with the chicks_____

Mix all the ingredients except the tater chips together; pour into a casserole dish. Sprinkle the chips on top and bake at 450 degrees for 20 minutes. This is enough chicken feed for 8 hungry Roosters and Hens...

PO' BOY CASSEROLE

1 lb of hamburger meat

1 small can of whole kernel corn

1 can cream mushroom soup

1 can cream chicken soup

1 medium onion (diced)

1 package thin egg noodles (cooked)

8 oz. sour cream

8-10 butter crackers (crumbled)

_____Po' Boy's Mix-n-Match_____

Brown meat & onions together - Combine all ingredients except for crackers and pour in a 2 quart baking dish. Top with crackers and Bake 30 minutes at 350 degrees.

Cass-er-roll dat over here...

Hillbilly Blue Ribbon Corn Casserole

1 can of whole kernel corn

1 can of cream-style corn

4 Tbs. all purpose flour

2 eggs- beaten

1 cup of milk

1 stick of butter- melted

2 Tbs. sugar

$\frac{1}{4}$ cup of green bell pepper-diced

$\frac{1}{4}$ tsp of salt – $\frac{1}{4}$ tsp of black pepper

_____This will win a blue ribbon at a Hillbilly fair_____

Combine all the ingredients in a large bowl; Pour it into a greased casserole dish and bake at 350 degrees for 1 $\frac{1}{2}$ hours.

Oh Shucks, this knocks the corn off the cob!

The Shipwrecked Casserole

4 medium taters- sliced

1 ½ lb. hamburger meat

1 onion-chopped

1 stalk of celery-chopped

1 cup of cooked rice

1 can of kidney beans

1 large can of maters

Salt & pepper to taste

_____S.O.S. this casserole is sinking fast!_____

Place taters on bottom of a greased casserole dish; season
with salt and pepper. Sprinkle onions and celery over top.
Add rice. Cover with beans. Place hamburger over beans;
pour maters over top and season with salt and pepper.
Bake at 350 degrees for 1 hour and 30 minutes. This will
feed 6 cast-a-way hillbillies on a deserted island.

Hillbilly Poke Chop & Tater Casserole

4 big poke chops (pork chops)

1 can of cream of mushroom soup

½ cup of sour cream

3 Tbs. of parsley flakes

3 medium taters, peeled and sliced

_____Let's poke some fun at the chops_____

Brown the chops. Mix soup and sour cream and parsley flakes together. Place taters in a greased casserole dish: place pork chops on top of them taters. Pour soup & sour cream mixture over top. Cover the casserole dish with foil or lid. Bake at 400 degrees for 1 hour and 15 minutes. Feeds 4 little piggies

Whut's dat oinking noise comin' from the oven?

Happy as a Hawg Casserole

1lb. of your favorite whole hawg sausage (mild or hot)

1 cup of rice

2 cans of chicken-gumbo soup

1 ½ soup cans of water

2 cups of celery (diced)

_____Let's make your hungry hawg happy_____

Brown sausage: drain. Brown rice in same pan with sausage until golden brown; mix all the ingredients and pour into a casserole dish. Bake covered at 350 degrees for 1 hour. Dat will make six little hungry hawgs happy.

Bring on the cathead biscuits or cornbread….Oink!

Upside-Down Casserole

1 lb. Hamburger meat

3 cups of cooked macaroni -drained

1 8oz package of grated cheddar cheese

$\frac{3}{4}$ cup of milk

1 8oz. can of tomato sauce

$\frac{1}{2}$ cup minced onion

3 tbsp. butter

1 tsp. salt

$\frac{1}{4}$ tsp. pepper

$\frac{1}{4}$ tsp. garlic salt

3 eggs beaten

_____Flip dat stuff up right_____

Cook onions in butter until tender; add beef and brown; stir in salt, pepper, garlic salt and tomato sauce-spread meat mixture in a 2 quart casserole dish; toss in macaroni with cheese; spoon onto beef mixture. Press down. Mix eggs and milk; pour over macaroni. Bake at 350 degrees for 1 hour and 30 minutes. Let stand for 15 minutes. INVERT onto a large platter. Feeds 6 upside-down hillbillies.

Apple-Tater & Sausage Casserole

8 of your favorite sausage patties (mild or hot)

2-3 large sweet taters (cooked)

2 cups of fresh sliced apples (Red or tart green apples)

$\frac{1}{4}$ cup of brown sugar

$\frac{1}{4}$ tsp. of ground cinnamon

_____Drown dat pig in apples & taters_____

Cook sausage; drain and place apples and sweet taters in casserole dish; sprinkle with the sugar and cinnamon. Place sausage patties on top and cover with foil or lid and bake at 375 degrees for 30 minutes. Uncover and bake for additional 15 minutes. Dat'll feed 6 hungry hillbillies

Maw's Mac-n- Sausage Casserole

1 lb. pork sausage (mild or hot)

1 (7oz.) package of macaroni-cooked and drained

1 medium onion-chopped

2 (8oz.) cans of mater sauce

1 Tbs. Worcestershire sauce

Salt & Pepper to taste

_____Let's Mac this Pig in the Mouth!_____

Brown sausage over low heat; add onion and cook for 5 minutes-drain. Combine sausage mixture, mater sauce, Worcestershire sauce, salt and pepper and mix it well. Combine macaroni and mixture and mix it well. Pour into a buttered 2 qt. casserole dish. Bake at 350 degrees for 30 minutes. Feeds 4 Hillbillies.

Hillbilly Corn Chip Casserole

2 lb Hamburger Meat

1 large onion

1 large can of mater sauce

2 Tbs. chili powder

2 tsp salt

1 cup if grated cheddar cheese

1 bag of corn chips

Water as desired

_____Chip in on this casserole_____

Brown hamburger meat with onions. Add mater sauce, chili powder, salt and water and simmer for 10-15 minutes. Layer beef mixture, cheese, and corn chips in a 2 quart casserole dish. Bake at 350 degrees for 15 minutes or until cheese melts. It feeds 4 hillbillies.

Hillbilly Pepper Steak Casserole

1 ½ lbs of round steak

½ cup of your favorite BBQ sauce

2 Tbs. canola or veggie oil

2 Tbs. flour

1/8 tsp black pepper

½ medium onion; sliced

1 medium green bell pepper- cut into strips

1 large mater cut into chunks

_____Pepper up dat Steak!_____

Cut steak into strips; dip strips in flour and pepper. Brown strips in hot cookin' oil in a large skillet. Add onions, bell pepper, maters and BBQ sauce to steak. Cover; simmer for 1 hour or until steak is tender and sauce is thick. Feeds 4-5 Hungry Hillbillies

This will make a Hillbilly Chef out of you...

Hillbilly Family Favorite Casserole

1 lb. pork sausage (mild or hot)

1 can of whole kernel corn-drained

1 can of red kidney beans- drained

1 small onion-diced

¼ tsp of salt

_____Git your family together for some good grub_____
Brown sausage-drain; Add corn, beans, onions, and salt; cook for 5-6 minutes. Add some cornbread to the mix and they ain't nothin' finer- Feeds a Hillbilly family of 4

Dat's what I called dressin' up the family pig...Oink!

Cheese -N- Tater Casserole

6 medium unpeeled taters- scrubbed and thinly sliced

1 (13 oz) can of cream of mushroom soup

1 cup of cheddar cheese- grated

3 Tbs. butter or margarine

$\frac{3}{4}$ cup of milk

$\frac{1}{4}$ tsp salt

$\frac{1}{4}$ tsp black pepper

_____Let's get cheesy with our taters_____

Layer half of the taters, seasoning, cheese and soup in a greased casserole dish. Top with half of the butter. Lay down a second layer of taters, seasoning, and soup. Top with remaining butter. Take and pour milk over top. Cover dish and bake at 350 degrees for 1 hour or until them taters are tender; Remove the covering remaining cheese. Put bake in oven just long enough for cheese to melt. Feeds 6-8 hungry hillbillies.

You don't have to be cheesy to eat these taters, but it helps

Hillbilly Steak-n-Tater Casserole

1 lb of round steak- cut up

1 Tbs. flour

1 Tbs. canola or veggie oil

2 medium taters, peeled and sliced

$\frac{1}{2}$ diced onion

$\frac{1}{4}$ tsp salt

Dash of black pepper

1 tsp Chopped parsley

1 (8oz.) can of mater sauce

_____Make those taters taste like a T-Bone_____

Roll the steak in the flour; brown in cookin' oil. Put steak in a casserole dish. Add taters, onions, salt, pepper, and parsley. Pour the mater sauce over mixture; cover and bake in 350 degrees oven for 1 hour or until taters are tender. Makes 6 Hillbillies happy!

Country Cheesy Tater Casserole

1 large bag of country style hash browns

1 can of cream of chicken soup

2 cups of sour cream

2 cups of shredded cheddar cheese

2 cups of crushed corn flaked cereal

$\frac{1}{2}$ tsp of salt

$\frac{1}{4}$ tsp of ground black pepper

$\frac{1}{2}$ cup of green onions – sliced

$\frac{1}{4}$ cup of melted butter

_____Make them cheesy taters countryfied_____

Preheat oven to 375 degrees. Coat 13x9 casserole dish with cooking spray; in a large bowl, whisk together soup, sour cream, salt and pepper. Mix in cheese, hash browns and onions; mix well. Spoon evenly into casserole dish- in another bowl, mix together melted butter and cereal and set to the side. Bake uncovered for 45 minutes. Remove from the oven and sprinkle cereal mix over entire hash brown mixture and continue to bake for 30 minutes. Let stand for 5 minutes before serving; sprinkle the green onions of top...feeds 8 hungry hillbillies.

Cowboy Casserole

4-6 medium sliced Taters

1 sliced onion

1 can of kidney or pinto beans w/juice

1 can of mater soup

Strips of Applewood smoked bacon

_____Hey Hillbilly Gals, Round Your Cowboys Up!_____

Place layer of taters, onions and beans in casserole dish. Add soup and top off with bacon strips. Bake at 350 degrees for 1 hour or until taters are done- Feeds up to 6 hungry cow pokes…and that's no joke.

Rodeo up some cornbread… Hee Haw, Y'all

Big Oink Pork Chop Casserole

6 big oink pork chops

Salt & pepper

1 large can of baked beans

1 cup of chili sauce

1 can of mater soup

1 Tbs. of brown sugar

Dash of hot sauce

1 tsp Worcestershire sauce

1 large green bell pepper- seeded and cut into rings

_____Make Some Big Oinking Sounds_____

Brown chops on both sides; season to taste with salt & pepper. Place in a greased casserole dish. Mix beans, chili sauce, soup, sugar hot sauce and Worcestershire sauce; Spoon over chops; place green bell pepper rings on top. Bake at 375 degrees for 1 hour.

Hillbilly Cookbook Desserts

Everybody has a "Sweet Tooth." I think the term "sweet tooth" was coined by some good hillbilly mountain folks. As a hillbilly myself, I have heard all the jokes about us not having teeth or very little of them...well, who's counting anyway? Whether you have a full rack, half rack, one tooth, or going bare back, we all still have a sweet tooth for great desserts after a big hardy hillbilly meal. That's why I have put this section of fine desserts in my cookbook. I hope you, your family and the friends that come to visits you will enjoy. So now you can be the sweetheart of the hollow...Git out your bakin' pans, pie pans, or iron skillets and crank up the stove...it's time for that heavenly dessert.

Hillbilly Dave

Quick-A-Billy Cobbler

2 cups of fruit (Blackberries, Peaches, Strawberries)

1 cup of self-rising flour

1 cup of sugar

1 cup of milk

1/3 stick of melted butter

_____Wow, how simple is that for a hungry hillbilly_____

This is so quick and simple and the results are outrageously good...

Mix together the flour, sugar, milk and melted butter in a large bowl, grease a baking pan and pour the mixture in the baking pan, then drop the fruit in and put in a pre-heated oven 350 degrees for 1 hour...let stand and cool for a few minutes and add a big scoop of vanilla ice cream to your awesome cobbler and let it tickle your sweet tooth with this hillbilly delight.

Southern Sweet Tater Cobbler

2 cups of sliced sweet taters

1 cup of self-rising flour

1 cup of milk

½ cup of sugar

½ cup of brown sugar

1 Tbsp. of cinnamon

½ stick of melted butter

_____Get ready to gobble some tater cobbler_____

Mix all the ingredients except the sweet taters in a large bowl. Pour mix into a well-greased large baking pan….place the finely sliced sweet taters in the mix in a nice even layer…Bake at 350 degrees for 1 hour….Bring out the vanilla ice cream and make it scream with a scoop or two.

Big Buford's Butternut Squash Pie

1 ½ cups of Butternut Squash, mashed

1 ½ cups of sugar

4 eggs

1 Tbs. vanilla

1 tsp. cinnamon

½ stick of melted butter

Pecans

Pinch of salt

_____Buford went nuts over this pie_____

Mix the squash, sugar, vanilla flavoring, salt, melted butter, cinnamon, and beat in the four eggs and mix well. Pour into two unbaked pie shells. Bake at 350 degrees until golden brown…Top with pecans and……

Squash this down for a hillbilly dessert!

Hen House Egg Pie

4 large eggs

1 cup of sugar

1 cup of milk

$\frac{1}{2}$ tsp. vanilla

_____Dat will make you want to cluck_____

Beat the rooster out of them eggs. Add the sugar, milk, and vanilla flavoring. Pour into an unbaked pie shell. Bake at 350 degrees for 30 minutes…let it cool, slice and serve.

Dat will make a hillbilly rooster stand up and crow!

Aunt Angel's Apple Glazed Cake

3 cups of chopped fresh red apples

1 cup of chopped pecans

1 $\frac{1}{2}$ of cooking oil-canola or veggie oil

2 cups of sugar

3 eggs

3 cups of plain flour

1 tsp. baking soda

1 tsp. salt

2 tsp, vanilla

_____Make this cake have a glazed look about it_____

(Glaze: 1 cup of brown sugar packed, $\frac{1}{4}$ cup of milk, 1 stick of butter...bring to boil for 2 $\frac{1}{2}$ minutes.)

Cake directions; Mix oil, sugar, and eggs until well blended. Add flour, baking soda, and salt (makes a stiff batter). Add 3 cups of apples, vanilla, and pecans. Bake at 325 degrees for 1 hour. Take cake out of oven and pour the glaze over it and let stand for 2 hours to absorb the glaze....dat will make your sweet tooth holler for more!

STRAWBERRY CREAM CHEESE COBBLER

1 Stick of butter ($\frac{1}{2}$ cup)

1 egg - lightly beaten

1 cup milk

1 cup all-purpose flour

1 cup of sugar

2 tsp baking powder

$\frac{1}{2}$ tsp salt

2 Quarts of Strawberries (capped & washed)

4 oz. cream cheese

_____Down at the Strawberry Patch_____

Pre- Heat oven 350 degrees- melt butter and pour into a 9x13 glass baking dish. In a bowl mix together egg, milk, flour, sugar, baking powder and pour over butter in baking dish (Do Not Stir). Add strawberries in a single layer as much as possible, sprinkle diced cream cheese over strawberries, place in oven and bake for 45 minutes or until top is golden brown and the edges are bubbling- crust rises up and around strawberries but will still peak out at the top.

*** Add a scoop of vanilla ice cream that will make you scream...for more!

Sunrise Cheese Cake Stuffed Strawberries

1 package of large strawberries

1 large container of extra creamy whipped cream

1 package of cream cheese (softened)

1 $\frac{1}{2}$ tsp. vanilla extract

1 box of cheesecake flavored pudding

Zip Lock Freezer bag

_____Stuff dem strawberries with hillbilly heaven_____

Wash strawberries, cut an X in the top of each strawberry and allow them to dry and chill them in the fridge for a few minutes. Fold together whipped cream and pudding till blended. Slowly add cheese cream and vanilla extract. Place mixture in the zip lock bag and chill for 30 minutes.. Remove bag from refrigerator and snip the corner of the bag off and pipe into the cut strawberries.

PUNKIN PATCH PUFFS

1 ½ cups of sifted flour

3 tsp Baking flour

¾ tsp salt

½ cup of sugar

½ tsp cinnamon

½ tsp nutmeg

4 tsp vegetable oil + fruit juice to equal ¼ cup

1 cackler (egg) well beaten

½ cup of pumpkin (canned)

½ cup of milk

½ cup of raisins

_____PUFF THE MAGIC HILLBILLY_____

1. Sift dry ingredients together. Stir in oil. Add egg, pumpkin, and milk. Stir in raisins.
2. Spray muffin pan with non-stick spray or use paper liners.
3. Pour in batter and bake at 400 degrees for 15-20 minutes.

Dat will make ya 9 lip smackin' muffins

Hillbilly Easy Peanut Butter Fudge

1 cup of peanut butter (smooth or chunky)

2 cups of sugar

½ cup of milk

1 tsp. vanilla flavoring

_____Simple as hillbilly arithmetic_____

Bring sugar & milk to a boil (about 2-3 minutes)

Remove from heat and stir in the peanut butter and vanilla

Place in a greased pan and let it cool. Cut it up in cubes and enjoy!

Dat will have your sweet tooth counting backwards...wee doggie!

Paw-Paw's Favorite Pecan Cobbler

1 cup of pecans

6 Tbs. of butter

1 ½ cups of sugar

1 ½ cups of brown sugar-packed

1 ½ cups of hot water

1 ½ cups of self-rising flour

2/3 cups of milk

1 tsp of vanilla

_____Paw-Paw goes nuts over this cobbler_____

Preheat oven to 350 degrees. Add butter to a 9x13 casserole dish or baking pan; melt butter in oven. Once butter in melted sprinkle pecans over butter- In a large bowl mix flour, sugar, milk, and vanilla stir to combine but do not over mix. Pour batter over melted butter and pecans- do not stir; sprinkle the brown sugar evenly over batter- do not stir; pour hot water over mixture- do not stir...Bake for 30-35 minutes or until it's golden brown.

Dat will make a Hillbilly's sweet tooth go nuts!

150

Mountain Mama's Pecan Pie

1 cup of pecans

3 eggs

1 cup of sugar

1 cup syrup (light or dark)

$\frac{1}{4}$ cup of butter

1 tsp vaniller

1 (9 inch) pie shell

_____Work it Mountain Mama!_____

Beat the eggs slightly... Mix syrup, butter, vaniller, and salt together...Mix in pecans last...Pour into unbaked pie shell and bake @ 400 degrees for 15 minutes, then cut down the heat to 350 degrees and bake for 30 minutes more.

Dat will make yo' sweet tooth sparkle...

Old Apple Orchard Tacos

1 large can of Apple Pie filling

1 pack of Soft Taco shells

Cinnamon

Sugar

1 can of whip topping

1 jar of caramel topping

_____Apple Up Your Tacos_____

Fold your taco shell in half and brown in skillet (both sides) with canola or veggie oil until light brown. In a pan or flat dish mix cinnamon and sugar together and coat both sides of the fried shell with that mixture. Fill taco shell with the apple filling and put whip cream on next and drizzle the caramel topping on top...

WOW! What a Taco

Maw and Paw's Peach-n-Berry Cobbler

1 (16oz.) package of frozen sliced peaches (don't thaw)

1 cup of frozen blackberries (don't thaw)

$\frac{3}{4}$ cup of sugar and 2 Tbs. of sugar

1 tsp of grated lemon rinds

1 tsp corn starch

1 cup of milk

1 heaping cup of self rising flour

$\frac{1}{2}$ cup of melted butter

_____Gobble down a Hillbilly cobbler_____

Mix together the frozen peaches, blackberries, $\frac{3}{4}$ cups of sugar, cornstarch, and lemon zest; place in a greased baking dish. Combine flour and 2 Tbs. of sugar in a large bowl; make a hole in the center. Stir together the milk and butter and add to the dry ingredients; stir until moistened. Spoon over the fruit mixture making sure it's spread evenly. Bake at 400 degrees for 55 minutes to 1 hour until crust is a golden brown. Top dat baby off with some vanilla ice cream and you will scream for more.

Ole Snuffy's Snickers Pie

1 shortbread or graham cracker crust
6 regular size Snickers candy bars or 24 fun size bars
18 regular marshmallows
1/4 cup milk or half and half
8 oz. frozen whipped topping
1/2 cup chopped dry roasted peanuts
chocolate syrup ice cream topping

_____Holy Snickers, Hillbilly!_____

Place the candy bars, marshmallows and milk or half and half
in a large mixing bowl and microwave for about 2 minutes on
high. Remove and stir well. If it has not all melted, microwave
for about 30 seconds more. If you don't have a microwave,
you can also melt it over a double boiler on the stove. When it
is all melted stir in the peanuts and allow to cool slightly.
When it has cooled, stir in the frozen whipped topping and
blend. Pour into the pie shell. Freeze the pie for at least 4
hours or overnight before serving.
Remove from freezer and drizzle with chocolate syrup before
serving.
Serve with whipped cream and a cherry!

Paw-Paw's Pear Fritters

$\frac{1}{2}$ cup of milk

1 cackler (egg) slightly beaten

2 tsp. sugar

1 tsp. of ground cinnamon

1 cup of sour cream

1 cup of self rising flour

2 peeled Pears- cored

Veggie or Canola Oil for frying

_____Fast Fixin' them Fritters_____

Whisk together milk, egg, sugar, cinnamon, and sour cream- add flour and set it aside.

Slice the cored pears into rings...Heat oil in skillet. Dip rings into batter and put in hot oil...Fry them babies up until golden brown. Top with vaniller ice cream and sprinkle with cinnamon-sugar mixture, and powdered sugar. Drizzle some maple syrup on them...Make you want to slap your paw-paw!

Kissin' Cousin's Coconut Carmel Pie

7 oz bag of coconut flakes

1 cup of pecans- chopped

16 oz. Cool Whip

1 (12 oz) jar of caramel topping

1 stick of butter

1 can of sweetened condensed milk

8 oz of cream cheese- softened

2 graham cracker pie crust

_____It's better than kissin' your cousin_____

Melt butter in large skillet. Add nuts and coconut; cook until light browned. Set aside to cool. Beat the cream cheese while gradually adding the canned milk, mix well. Stir in Cool Whip; Divide $\frac{1}{4}$ of the mixture into each pie crust and drizzle $\frac{1}{4}$ jar caramel topping. Sprinkle coconut-pecan mixture on top; repeat layers - Store pies in refrigerator to cool. Cut, eat, and enjoy!

Hillbilly Heaven Zucchini Bread

1 1/2 cups all purpose flour
1 tsp. baking powder
1/2 tsp. salt
1/2 tsp. baking soda
1 tsp. cinnamon
1 cup sugar
1 cup shredded zucchini
2 eggs
1/2 cup vegetable oil
1 tsp. lemon zest
1 tsp. vanilla

_____GRAB YA LOAF OR TWO_____

1/2 cup pecans or walnuts, chopped
Preheat oven to 350 degrees,
Mix first 5 ingredients in a separate bowl. In a mixing bowl beat
together sugar, eggs, oil, zucchini and lemon zest. Add vanilla. Gradually
add flour mixture. Fold in nuts.
Pour into a well greased loaf pan. Bake at 350 degrees for 45 to 50
minutes. Remove from oven and cool for about 10 minutes before
turning it out.
Cinnamon Honey Cream Cheese Spread
1 8oz block of cream cheese, softened (I used light)
3 Tbs. honey
1/2 tsp. cinnamon

Hillbilly Sweet & Spicy Popcorn

If you like to get spicy & sweet with your date, wait 'til you grab some of this...

9 cups cooked popcorn

3 Tbs. butter

$\frac{1}{4}$ tsp cinnamon

$\frac{1}{4}$ tsp nutmeg

$\frac{1}{2}$ tsp of sugar

_____Hillbilly corn gone wild, sweet & spicy_____

Melt butter. Add sugar and spices. Pour over popped corn, stir well. Dump it in your favorite bowl...Simple enough!

Thank my Hillbilly corn; its movie night...Hunny turn out the lights, it's show time!

Hillbilly Nanner Nut Bread

1 cup of mashed nanners (bananas)

2 cups of flour

$\frac{1}{2}$ tsp of bakin' soda

2 tsp of bakin' powder

$\frac{3}{4}$ tsp of salt

$\frac{1}{2}$ cup of sugar

1 egg- well beaten

$\frac{1}{4}$ Tbs. of lemon juice

1 cup of Chopped pecans or walnuts

_____Ain't nuttin' better than Hillbilly nanner bread_____

Mix dry ingredients; stir in $\frac{3}{4}$ cup of nuts. Mix nanners, eggs, and lemon juice; add to dry ingredients and stir well. Pour batter into a greased loaf pan; sprinkle remaining nuts on top. Bake for 1 hour at 350 degrees.

Whut a nanner delight!

Hillbilly Gorilla Bread

Forget the monkey business and bring out the Gorilla

3 cans of Southern Style Biscuits (not flakey)

1 cup sugar

1 cup of brown sugar

2 tsp cinnamon

1 stick of butter

Cup of pecans

_____Call in the Hillbilly Gorilla_____

Quarter up them canned biscuits. Place in a large zip-lock bag with cinnamon and sugar; Shake the monkey out of them. Put into a Bundt Pan (spray with non-stick oil); Melt butter and mix in the brown sugar. Pour over biscuits and sprinkle with pecans. Bake at 350 degrees for 25-30 minutes. Turn over Bundt pan on a safe surface and let the Gorilla out!

Hillbilly Cow Patties

$\frac{1}{2}$ Cup of peanut butter

2 cups of sugar

$\frac{1}{2}$ cup of milk

$\frac{1}{2}$ cup of butter

4 Tbs. cocoa

3 $\frac{1}{2}$ cups of quick oats

2 tsp of vanilla

_____Gotta watch what you are stepping in on the farm_____

Add butter, sugar, milk and coca in a medium sauce pan and bring to a boil for 1 minute...stir in peanut butter, oats, and vanilla and drop in patty shape clusters onto wax paper. Let cool before serving.

These will make a cow jealous

Mountain Mama's Raspberry Fritters

1 cup of raspberry jam (or your favorite flavor of jam)

1 tsp. vanilla

Bananas (sliced in small pieces)

Hazelnut spread

Dumpling wrappers

Water

_____FRITTER THIS! _____

Step one: Mix raspberry jam and vanilla together in a microwave safe bowl and microwave it on high for 1 minute.

Step Two: In separate little bowls have the raspberry jam mixture, hazelnut spread, bananas, and water ready.

Step 3: Spread Raspberry jam, hazelnut spread, and top it off with the sliced bananas on the dumpling wrap

Step 4: Take the water and rub around the edges of the wrapper for to seal...Fold the filled dumpling wrap over press around the edges to make the seal, take a fork and make ridges around the edges.

Step 5: In a large fryin' pan, add canola oil or peanut oil and fry fritters until golden brown.

Step 6: Sprinkle the tops of fritters with powder sugar.

Hillbilly Hint: Make some chocolate syrup to dip them suckers in...YUM!

HILLBILLY PUNKIN' BREAD

1 large can of Punkin' (pumpkin)

2/3 Cup of shortening

4 eggs

½ tsp baking powder

1 ½ tsp salt

1 tsp of cloves

2/3 cups of water

3 1/3 cup of flour

2 tsp baking soda

1 tsp cinnamon

2/3 cups of pecans

2/3 cups of raisins- chopped

2 2/3 cups of sugar

_____That Little Punk!_____

Cream thoroughly the sugar and the shortening...Add eggs and punkin' and water: beat well. Sift dry ingredients and nuts then add to mixture. Bake in a loaf pan well greased like a pig at the state fair for about 1 hour at 350 degrees.

Hillbillies can't live by bread alone, but this punkin' bread will make you try!

HILLBILLY COCKTAIL PUDDIN'

1 Can of fruit cocktail

2 cups of milk

1 large pack of instant vanilla puddin' mix

1 box of vaniller wafers

½ cup of pecans- chopped

_____Hillbillies love dat Puddin'_____

Mix puddin' according to the directions on the box – in a nice large glass bowl layer puddin' with fruit cocktail and vaniller wafers…Repeat layers and top with crushed vaniller wafers and use the pecans & cherries from the fruit cocktail to garnish with. Dat's easy enough!

Granny's Old Fashion Chocolate Pie

$\frac{1}{4}$ cup of cocoa

1 $\frac{1}{4}$ cup of sugar

$\frac{1}{2}$ cup of all purpose flour

2 cups of milk

4 egg yolks (save the whites for topping)

$\frac{1}{4}$ cup of butter

1 tsp vanilla flavoring

Dash of salt

1 nine inch pie shell (baked)

_____Put some Old Fashion taste in your hillbilly pie_____
Bake crust until golden brown. Combine sugar, flour, cocoa, and salt in a sauce pan and set aside. Mix milk and egg yolks and stir it in with mixture and add butter. Cook over medium heat-stirring constantly until mix thickens and comes to a boil. Remove from heat and stir in vanilla and put in crust. Use egg whites to make a meringue and put on top of pie. Note: add $\frac{1}{4}$ cup of sugar to each egg white and beat to it becomes fluffy. Put under broiler for a few seconds to let it get toasty brown on top. Let it set a few minutes before cutting and serving. Enjoy!

MOUNTAIN MAMA'S EASY PEACH COBBLER

4 cups of fresh peaches, peeled, pitted and diced
1 1/2 cups sugar, divided
1/2 cup of butter (1 stick)
1 cup of self rising flour
1 cup milk
1 1/2 tsp. cinnamon, divided
1 tsp. vanilla

_____Ain't dat just peachy_____

***You can substitute 2 (15 oz.) cans of sliced peaches, undrained for the fresh peaches

Place the peeled and diced peaches in bowl with 1/2 cup of sugar. Peaches are sweet naturally and don't require much sweetening.

In a 9"x13" baking pan, melt the butter.

Mix together the milk, self rising flour, 1 cup sugar, 1 tsp. vanilla and 1 tsp. cinnamon until smooth- Pour over the melted butter in the baking pan. DO NOT STIR.

Lay the peaches over the batter and DO NOT STIR. Sprinkle the top with the other 1/2 tsp. of cinnamon. Place in the oven and bake at 350 degrees for 50 to 55 minutes or until the top is brown.

This is best served warm with a scoop of vanilla ice cream or whipped cream!

166

CRAZY HOLLOW NUT CAKE

2 cups of plain flour

7 eggs

1 ½ cups of sugar

½ LB Butter

½ tsp salt

2 tsp vanilla

1 tsp almond extract

2 tsp baking powder

2 ½ cups of nuts...(pecans, almonds, or walnuts)

_____you'll go nuts over this cake!_____

Mix all the ingredients together, beat the far out of it on high for 5 minutes. Put in your favorite can pan and bake it for 1 hour at 325 degrees....Taste that and it will make you go crazy!

Aunt Pearl's Chocolate Chip Punkin' Delight

1 (15oz.) can of punkin (Pumpkin)

1 box of spice cake mix

2 eggs

¼ tsp cinnamon

1/3 cup of water

1 ½ cup of chocolate chips (milk chocolate)

_____Punkin never tasted this good!_____

Preheat oven to 350 degrees. Grease and flour ya up a Bundt pan. Mix punkin, cake mix, eggs, cinnamon, and water in a large bowl; beat for a couple of minutes until it's blended well. Stir in 1 cup of the chocolate chips. Pour into Bundt pan and bake for 40 minutes. Cool in pan for 15 minutes, then turn it over on a plate or cutting board and let the delight fall out. Melt the other ½ cup of chips in the microwave on high for 1 minute…stir and drizzle it on top of the delight.

Dat will make your sweet tooth happy!

Aunt Pearl's Icebox Peach Pie

1 can of Sliced Peaches (drain)

1 cup of sugar

1 cup of cold water

6 Tbs. cornstarch

4 tsp of lemon juice

Dash of salt

1 drop of almond flavoring

2 drops of yellow food coloring

1 drop of red food coloring

4 Tbs. apricot or orange jello mix (dry)

_____Make it Peachy!_____

Cook sugar, cornstarch, salt and water until thick and clear. Add lemon juice, flavorings and food colors. Add jello mix and let it cool. Put peaches in cooled sauce and mix well. Pour into 1 baked pie shell and refrigerate. Serve with Cool Whip topping on top.

Rowdy's Raspberry Peach Delight Cake

1 prepared Angel Food Cake- Cut in inch cubes

1 - 3oz. pkg. of Raspberry JELL-O

1 Cup of boiling water

1 Cup of cold water

1 can light Peaches

3 cups of milk

1 - (1.5oz.) of Vanilla Pudding

1 - 8oz. Cool Whip

_____Let's get rowdy with raspberries and peaches_____

Arrange cake cubes on bottom of a 9x13 pan or dish

Dissolve Jell-O in boiling water then stir in cold water

Pour Jell-O over cake; Arrange Peaches over Jell-O

Mix Milk and Vanilla Pudding spread over peaches-Top with cool whip. Refrigerate for 2 hours before cutting the cake.

APPLE ORCHARD CRUNCH

1 jar of cinnamon applesauce

$\frac{3}{4}$ cups sugar

1/8 cup of water

Mix these ingredients together in bottom of casserole dish then stir in the following ingredients...

$\frac{3}{4}$ cup plain flour

$\frac{3}{4}$ cups of uncooked oats

$\frac{1}{2}$ tsp baking soda

Pinch of salt

_____Git out of dat apple tree_____

This forms crumbly dough. Place on top of apple mixture and bake until bubbly for 45 minutes at 350 degrees.

Throw you a slab of vaniller ice cream on it....Wee Doggie!

Aunt Annie's Coconut Orange Cake!

For this delicious cake you will need:

1 orange cake mix and whatever ingredients it calls for (we used Duncan Hines)

1 cup flaked, sweetened coconut

<u>Frosting</u>

1 15 oz. can mandarin oranges do not drain and crushed

1 large instant vanilla pudding mix (dry, not prepared)

1 cup flaked, sweetened coconut

1 8 oz. frozen whipped topping, thawed

Preheat oven to 350 degrees.

_____Get yo' cake pan ready_____

Spray two 9 inch cake pans with nonstick baking spray.

Prepare cake mix according to package directions adding in 1 cup coconut.

Bake cakes according to times on package directions.

When the cake layers have cooled, make the frosting. In a mixing bowl, crush the mandarin oranges with their juices with an electric mixer. Stir in the instant pudding mix and coconut. Fold in the whipped topping. Mix well. Frost the cake layers.

If you want to garnish the top with the 5-6 of the mandarin orange slices, remove them before you crush the rest.

Refrigerate for at least a couple of hours.

172

Hillbilly Cocktail Cake

.2 cups self rising flour\

2 eggs

1 1/2 cups white sugar

1 (15 oz.) can of fruit cocktail, undrained

1 tsp. vanilla

1 tsp. cinnamon

Frosting

1/2 cup butter (1 stick)

1 cup evaporated milk

1/2 cup white sugar

1/2 cup brown sugar

1 tsp. vanilla

1 cup pecans, chopped

2 cups flaked coconut or a 7 oz. bag

_____Preheat oven to 350 degrees. _____

Mix the flour, eggs, sugar, fruit cocktail, vanilla and cinnamon together until well blended. Pour into a well greased 9"x13" baking pan. Place in the oven and bake for 30-35 minutes.

Near the end of the baking time, prepare the frosting. Place the butter, milk, white and brown sugars, vanilla in a medium sauce pan over medium heat. Bring to a boil and boil for 1 minute. Reduce the heat and add the pecans and coconut. Mix well.

Remove the cake from the oven. I like to take a fork or wooden skewer and poke just a few holes in the cake to allow some of the frosting to run down into the cake, but you don't have to do that step. Pour the frosting evenly over the warm cake. Make sure the coconut and pecans are evenly distributed.   **173**

Southern Fruit Tea

2 family size tea bags or 8 individual tea bags
4 cups boiling water
1 1/2 - 2 cups sugar (according to your taste)
1 (6 oz.) can frozen orange juice concentrate
1 (6 oz.) can frozen lemonade
1 cup pineapple juice
10 cups water
1 lemon, sliced in thin slices
1 lime, sliced in thin slices
1 orange, sliced in thin slices
1 cup maraschino cherries, drained (optional)

_____Better than moonshine_____

Boil the tea bags in the 4 cups of boiling water just until it boils. Turn off and cover too steep for at least 30 minutes.
In a gallon container (glass preferably) mix the warm tea with the sugar and stir to dissolve. Once the sugar is completely dissolved add the orange juice, lemonade, and pineapple juice. Stir to mix well. Add the 10 cups of water and stir again.
Make small cuts in the skin of the lemon, lime, and orange. Just light cuts not through to the skin. This releases the oils and flavor of the fruit. Slice all three in thin slices and float in the fruit tea. Add ice to completely fill the container and stir again. To make it really pretty you can float the maraschino cherries in it!

Hillbilly Hot Apple Cider

2 quarts of unsweetened apple cider

1 cup of sugar

1 cup of pineapple juice - unsweetened

2 fresh lemons- juice and pulp

1 orange- juice and pulp

6 cloves

3 cinnamon sticks

Dash of salt

_____Hot Cider on a Cold Day!_____

Simple directions: Bring all ingredients to a boil; reduce heat and simmer for 10-15 minutes. Note: you can use sweetened cider and pineapple juice, but eliminate the cup of sugar...

Pour ya a big cup of that and make your whistler dance a jig! Wee Doggie!

I hope ya loved these Hillbilly Recipes

Y'all come back and see me, you hear!

Hillbilly Dave